Korea's Historic Clans

Family Traditions of the Jongga

KOREA ESSENTIALS No. 19

Korea's Historic Clans

Family Traditions of the Jongga

Published in 2014 by Seoul Selection
B1 Korean Publishers Association Bldg., 6 Samcheng-ro, Jongno-gu, Seoul
110-190, Korea
Phone: (82-2) 734-9567
Fax: (82-2) 734-9562
Email: publisher@seoulselection.com
Website: www.seoulselection.com

ISBN: 978-89-97639-53-3 04080
ISBN: 978-89-97639-25-0 (set)
Printed in the Republic of Korea

Korea's Historic Clans

Family Traditions of the Jongga

KOREA FOUNDATION
한국국제교류재단

Seoul Selection

CONTENTS

Introduction 6

Chapter 1
Korean Family Names and the Meaning of Jongga 12
The History of Family Names | Confucianism and the Human Ideal in the Joseon Dynasty | The Jongga and Confucianism

Chapter 2
The Four Rituals That Give People Lives of Dignity 26
Gwanrye, Coming-of-Age Ceremony: First of the Four Rituals | Honrye, Traditional Wedding Ceremony: A Life Event to Be Treasured | Sangrye, Traditional Funeral: Saying Goodbye to Parents Whose Duty Is Done | Jerye, Ancestral Rites: Lifelong Responsibility of the Family Head

Chapter 3
Food Culture of the Jongga: From the Mouth to the Heart 48
The Role and Significance of Food in Jongga | Miryang Son Clan, Son Seong-jeung Jongga: Delicacies of the Richest Jongga in Gyeongsangnam-do | Papyeong Yun Clan, Yun Jeung Jongga: First Prize in a National Jongga Food Competition | Gyeongju Yi Clan, Yi Hang-bok Jongga: Soybean Paste Passed Down for Five Hundred Years

Chapter 4
Jongtaek, the House That Generations Have Called Home 64
The Characteristic of a Jongtaek | Munhwa Ryu Clan Gonsangun Jongga: Unjoru, One of the Three Most Propitious Sites in South Korea | Pungsan Ryu Clan, Ryu Seong-ryong Jongga: Yangjindang and Chunghyodang | Wolseong Son Clan, Sonso Jongga: A House That Prince Charles Admired

Chapter 5
Learning: The Teaching and Practice of Moral Principles 86

The Significance of Learning in Traditional Society | Education at the Jongga | Gyeongju Choi Clan Saseonggong Jongga: Self-Discipline and Sympathy | Daegu Seo Clan Seo Seong Jongga: Summoning the Courage to Seek Out Opportunity | Goseong Yi Clan, Yi Myeong Jongga: Sacrificing Everything for the Nation

Appendix
Information 108

Delving Deeper

- Separated from Her Husband by the Korean War, She Still Took Care of the Jongga 24
- Saving the Only Heir of the Six Martyred Ministers 46
- Handing Down Knowledge Instead of Money 62
- Jongga Where Children Are Raised to Be Courteous 84

Introduction

The sturdy doors of the *jongga*—which had been kept shut for centuries, are wide open at long last. It's now possible to learn about the family customs that have accumulated over the tumultuous 20th century, as well as the five centuries of the Joseon Dynasty that came before. Of all the changes that the *jongga* have understood in modern times, this must be the greatest. The *jongga* contain the places where ancestors spent their days and the private spaces where generations of their descendants lived their lives, and never before have their secrets been told.

You can now experience the unique *jongga* lifestyle, something that is unique to Korea. Guests at these homes can eat food

prepared by the woman of the house, sleep in the men's quarters, and hear stories that are imbued with the food, architecture, history, family values, and education of the *jongga*. When Queen Elizabeth II and her son Prince Charles visited Korea, the first place they went was a *jongga*; this change shows us how valuable the *jongga* are.

Korean dictionaries define *jongga* as a large house that is passed down to the eldest son of the family. According to *Zhu Xi's Family Rituals*, a Chinese book of etiquette and rituals written in the 12th century, the *jongga* is the greatest house in a family that is handed down from the original founder—the person who originated the family name—to the eldest son in each generation. In

Gyeongsangbuk-do alone, there are around 120 such houses, with countless more around Korea, each with their own distinctive regional characteristics. However, there is more to *jongga* culture than bloodline alone. The *jongga* is the means by which Confucian culture has been transmitted. It is an emotional haven and a spiritual compass, providing an identity not only for the members of the family but for the Korean people as a whole.

Even in Korea today, the family head and his wife, who are charged with caring for the *jongga*, are tasked with performing ancestral rites in the family shrine at the appropriate time, providing guests with a warm welcome, and maintaining harmony both in the family and in the larger community through the thoughtful service that characterizes their lives. These unique features of Korean family culture in general, and *jongga* in particular, were behind the selection of Hahoe Village in Andong and Yangdong Village in Gyeongju as UNESCO World Heritage sites in 2010.

As in many other parts of the world, the age of the nuclear family has dawned in Korea, with the exception of the *jongga*; after all, a dynamic society cannot cling to tradition forever. But during Korea's biggest holidays, family members living far apart congregate at the *jongga*, which represents the most important family house, as well as its spiritual center. They gather together to catch up on one another's lives and to find hope and courage. In Korea, family still has a broader meaning than it does in the West.

Family is a universal human concept, but the manifestation of this concept varies with each culture. By observing the families in a given society, we can learn something about the mindset of the people who belong to that society. Stepping through the open gate of the *jongga*, we find a pattern of life that these families have stubbornly held onto. This pattern can help us better understand this unique aspect of Korean culture, as well as aiding us in reflecting on what is missing from the lives we live today. As the

essence of Korean family culture, *jongga* culture is not merely a thing of the past—it is also part of Korea's present, and its future.

Some of the *jongga* have endured for hundreds of years and they still carry their traditions into the present day. Reviewing the history of the *jongga* and examining what they are today will teach us things about the Korean spirit that cannot be perceived from the outside.

"Lead people by means of regulations and keep order among them through punishments, and the people will evade them and will lack any sense of shame.

Lead people through moral force and keep order among them through rites (禮), and they will have a sense of shame and will also correct themselves."

– *Analects*, Confucius

1 Chapter One

KOREAN FAMILY NAMES AND THE MEANING OF JONGGA

The History of Family Names

"Which clan of the family are you from? What branch of the clan is it? Well, what generation are you? Where is your hometown?"

This kind of conversation is sometimes heard when Koreans exchange business cards. Even today, the family name a Korean is born with expresses their status, both past and present. The further back their family tree can be traced, the more credit society gives them. If two people with the same family name learn that they are from the same clan of that family as well, they are more likely to feel a sense of kinship.

However, family names in Korea are different from other countries. There are fewer family names in Korea than there are in other countries, meaning that far more Koreans share each of these names. As a result, it is completely impossible to distinguish someone by his or her family name alone.

Family Names from the Three Kingdoms to Joseon

A simple explanation to this riddle can be found by looking at the history of family names in Korea. Yi Deuk-seon, 81, head of the Yean Yi clan in Asan, Chungcheongnam-do and a distinguished Confucian scholar, explains how Koreans came to have family names in addition to their given names:

> You can see this in history texts such as *Samguksagi* (Historical Record of the Three Kingdoms) and *Samgukyusa* (Legends and History of the Three Kingdoms). Jumong, founder of Goguryeo, used the family name 'Go.' Onjo, who established the kingdom of Baekje, went by the family name 'Buyeo' since he was from

Suryubdo, a wall mural found in a tomb of Goguryeo period (37 B.C.–A.D. 668) describes archery. One of the first indigenous last names recorded in Korean history belongs to the progenitor of Goguryeo, Go Jumong, famous for his mastery of archery.

Taejo Wang Geon, the founder of Goryeo

the Buyeo bloodline. Hyeokgeose, who founded Silla, had the indigenous Korean name 'Bak.' That's why there are those legends about the Silla kings alternating between the three names 'Bak,' 'Seok,' and 'Kim.'"

But family names were not widely used in the Three Kingdoms period and appear to have been largely limited to the royal family and the aristocracy. The various clans (closely related groups sharing the same family name) began to be associated with particular "hometowns," or places of origin, under Taejo Wang Geon, the founder of Goryeo. King Taejo (r. 918–943) granted names to powerful families as part of his attempt to unify the peninsula. While, up until this point, family names had only been associated with the royalty and the nobility, Taejo gave Goryeo's people family names that corresponded to their respective hometowns, and also provided them with land on which they could make a living. This is why many of these clans are named after the land that they were given. The clans built *jongga* on the richest part of the land given to them, and as their descendants multiplied, towns known as jipseongchon appeared that were full of people sharing the same name.

In the *Sejongsilrokjiriji* (Geography Section of the Annals of King Sejong's Reign), a book published by the court of Joseon (the kingdom that succeeded Goryeo), 250 such family names were recorded. This number increased to 277 in *Donggukyeojiseungnam* (Augmented Survey of the Geography of Korea). Even though family names spread in this way through the bureaucrats who ruled the country, 40 percent of Koreans still lacked a family name at the close of the Joseon Dynasty.

The picture shows U.S. bombardment of North Korean City Wonsan during the Korean War.

Fate of Family Names in Modern History

It was only when the census registration law took effect in 1909 that it everyone was legally required to have both a family name and a clan. At that point, most people reported themselves as being Kim, Yi, or Bak (Park)—which were already common family names at that point—creating a peculiar situation in which a handful of names represented the bulk of the population. On top of that, many families' records were scattered during the wars that followed and the division of the peninsula.

In modern Korea, many relatives live far away from each other, making it harder to detect the bond that family names represent. However, given that some people will still habitually inquire about one's ancestry, there are traces that still remain of the huge significance that family names once carried. This becomes even clearer when considering the pivotal role that *jongga* played in families when subjected to Confucian ideals during the Joseon Dynasty.

Confucianism and the Human Ideal in the Joseon Dynasty

Portrait of Confucius

Confucianism was the ideology on which the Joseon Dynasty was established. Indeed, it was the strength of Confucianism's spiritual culture that enabled the Joseon Dynasty to endure for 500 years. Confucianism is an ideology that is at once spiritual and practical; it emphasizes morality, justice, and virtue, but also displays a scholarly component that teaches the principles and norms for proper conduct.

Under Confucianism, the peak of human development is the virtuous scholar, known as the *seonbi*. The scholar pursued his studies to attain the benevolence and righteousness advocated by Mencius, the Chinese Confucian thinker. This righteousness underlies an ethical system that is based on the so-called three bonds and five relationships, concepts that are derived from human relationships. In the view of Joseon thinkers, the reason for human existence is to be found in human relationships, with loyalty being a critical element of these relationships. This loyalty is a necessary virtue not only between king and vassal but also between teacher and student, parents and children, husband and wife, and between friends.

Key Virtues of a Seonbi

The most important virtues that scholars were expected to possess were honesty, discipline, and patience. Honesty was something on which scholars would stake their honor, and sometimes even their life. Discipline, or the ability to suppress instincts and desires and delay gratification, was demanded not only in everyday life and human relationships but also academic rigor. Finally, patience was the virtue required for one to understand the reason for and the value of controlling one's desires. To the scholar, discipline was inseparable from patience. By possessing these virtues, the scholar was able both to attain knowledge and simultaneously to put it into practice. The *jongga* was the place where the ideals of the *seonbi* were to be pursued. It also served as a kind of school at which the young were raised according to these same ideals.

Dosanseowon is where many *seonbi* of *jongga* went to improve their minds as well as studies.

The Jongga and Confucianism in Joseon Society

As the founding ideology of the Joseon Dynasty, Confucianism was deeply rooted not only in academic studies but also in society as a whole, even serving as the conceptual foundation of the *jongga*. Confucianism emphasizes that the family is the fundamental unit of which the nation as a whole is composed, and demands that both the family and the nation be administered according to the principles of loyalty and filial piety. It viewed the nation and the family as being identical in terms of the principles by which they were to be maintained and governed.

The ideology of Joseon focused on the family, regarding all members as being part of a single unit and everyone else as an

Jongmyojere, or ancestral rites at Jongmyo. Nearly thirty rites were held annually at Jongmyo during Joseon Dynasty but now it's observed once a year in the first Sunday of May, and lead by Jeonju Yi clan, which was the family of former Joseon royalties. It's open for public view.

outsider. Accordingly, all the individual members of the family had to work together to achieve the unit's collective goals; even with the accumulation and disposition of wealth, decisions were made at the family level rather than by individual members. If the other family members wanted something, it was the duty of individual members to provide, and if a family member got into trouble with an outsider, the family members were supposed to gladly come to their aid. Family members undertook and continued economic activity and started their own families in accordance with the expectations of the larger family. Behind all these actions was the imperative that the family must be preserved.

The Meaning of Jongga

People today are often unfamiliar with the terminology associated with *jongga*. Put in simple language, a *jongga* is a bloodline begun by a single ancestor that serves as a foundation for a household passed down to the eldest son of each generation. A greater *jongga*, or *daejongga*, is one that is passed down from the clan founder to the eldest sons without exception. For some of these greater *jongga*, the lineage can be traced back over 1,000 years. Lesser *jongga*, or *sojongga*, are created when a secondary clan founder breaks away from the greater *jongga*. The status of being deemed a secondary founder was bestowed upon those whose embodiments of *seonbi* values was unrivalled or whose contributions to Joseon society were especially significant, typically those individuals who have saved the nation from calamity or whose remarkable accomplishments in learning earned them the reputation of being a spiritual teacher for the nation. In such cases, the government decrees that their memorial tablets are never to be removed from the family shrine.

During the Joseon Dynasty, each family maintained a shrine in which they kept the memorial tablets of deceased ancestors, going back four generations. The royal family maintained memorial tablets for the king's ancestors at Jongmyo Shrine, while the memorial tablets of the nation's spiritual leaders were housed at Munmyo Shrine in Seonggyungwan in Seoul. For the 500 years of the Joseon Dynasty, Munmyo contained the memorial tablets of 18 great sages whose teachings were regarded as the spiritual foundation of Korean society.

Individual in Joseon Dynasty

The people of the Joseon Dynasty did not think of themselves as individuals, but rather as intermediaries between their ancestors and their descendants. They were the conduit that transmitted the teachings and ideology of their ancestors to their descendants. Because of their reverence for the spiritual lessons and teachings of their ancestors, they went to great lengths to preserve the writings containing their ancestors' philosophy that had been handed down from generation to generation. They would conceal these

The head family descended from Toegye's grandson, Dongam Yi Young-do

A typical *jesa* (ancestral rite) table, which in this case is set up for Chuseok (the Autumn Harvest Festival).

documents and letters underneath tiles on their roof or behind a plaster wall so that they would not be lost in the event of a fire, seeing these spiritual teachings as even more valuable than the family fortune. Indeed, poverty was often regarded as evidence of a scholar's integrity.

The idealistic image of the scholar sometimes clashed with the reality of everyday life. Many *jongga* ran into difficulties because they did not have sufficient financial means to conduct the numerous ancestral rituals and to properly entertain guests, a constant presence. However, the heads of these families—or *jongson*, the eldest living son the main lineage, and his wife, *jongbu* had deep respect and pride for their heritage and treasured their roles as the preservers of tradition. Hence they were able to endure economic hardship. They were able to maintain a dignified lifestyle thanks to the respect, encouragement, and material assistance they received from many members of their clan.

Jongga and the Significance of an Heir

Jongga households eagerly looked forward to the emergence of a prominent male figure in the family, whether this was the eldest son or someone else in the clan. They showed particular enthusiasm for the son of gifted family members, and they also searched for children inside the clan who could be raised into talented individuals who would serve the nation with distinction and bring glory to the clan. This is shown by the fact that, when the head of the *jongga* had no son, the family would seek out an intellectually talented boy to adopt, regardless of how distantly related he might be. They thought that the *jongga* prospered thanks to talented individuals who excelled in learning and virtue, and that such individuals would follow in the footsteps of their ancestors to achieve greatness. Thus, the values of a *jongga* household did not deal with the present alone, but instead connected the past to the future. This mindset devoted energy to the formation, development, and eventual decline not only of individuals and individual families but of the clan as a whole.

Koreans during the Joseon Dynasty believed that they were the ones who passed down the life and the spirit of their ancestors to their descendants. Under the *jongga*'s historical understanding, the present condition of individuals was the product of their past (the lives and thinking of their ancestors, and the history of the clan), and the spirit of the past was transmitted to the future through the proper education and upbringing of their children.

Separated from Her Husband by the Korean War, She Still Took Care of the Jongga

This is the story of a woman who looked after the jongga from the time she was 26 in place of her husband, the head of the family, who was unable to leave North Korea

On Children's Day, Kim Hu-ung, who lives in Gagu-ri, Waryong-myeon, in Andong, North Gyeongsang Province, doesn't have any grandchildren to look after. On Parent's Day, she has no children to buy carnations for her. Kim is the wife of the 14th son in the line of Kim Eon-gi (also known as Yu Il-jae), a renowned scholar and educator during the reign of King Seonjo of the Joseon Dynasty.

Hu-ung lost her only son to measles at the age of two, half a century ago. At the time, her in-laws reassured her that she could have another son, but she never had the chance to do so. After the Korean War, she and her husband Kim Yong-jin were forced to lived apart: Hu-ung was in the South, and Yong-jin in the North.

Five years ago, Hu-ung's ailing father-in-law, whom she had been looking after, passed away at the age of 99. Her sisters-in-law, whom she had raised like her own children, had already started their own families. Since her husband was gone, her brother-in-law ended up taking responsibility for the 18 annual ancestral rites that she had once done.

When Hu-ung finally managed to see her husband after 54 years, he already had his own family in North Korea. Now, the only things left for her to take care of are the buildings of the *jongga*, now covered in cobwebs; the souls of the family's ancestors, whose memorial tablets are kept at the family shrine; and her own body, now aged and infirm. Hu-ung is perhaps the last representative of the traditional Korean ideal of the woman, who is supposed to take care of her family even after losing her husband and children.

Japanese colonial government forced Koreans to change their names to Japanese style, which was unacceptable to people of *jongga*. Many fought in retaliation, like Kim Hu-ung's husband.

The Kim Eon-gi *jongga* in Andong is a clay-colored house with tiles on the roof. Though it does not have a wall or raised gate, it has the original form of a traditional Korean house. It even has a mill with a thatched roof. This is where Hu-ung had to grind the rice and barley, as well as the rice cake powder for the ancestral rites.

When I opened the inner gate on the west side of the women's quarters, the old woman hobbled down into the courtyard to greet me, propping herself up with a cane. When I bowed to greet her, she returned the bow despite her back pain. Though her back is bent and her hair is white, she carries herself with a dignity acquired during the years she spent as the *jongbu*, the mistress of an aristocratic family.

"Don't you feel lonely being here by yourself?" I asked.

"Lonely? Not at all. I've always lived this way."

"I heard that you saw your husband at Mountain Kumgang last year [2003]."

"We were separated when I was 26 and he was 25, so it was 54 years since we had seen each other. I'm just grateful that he's still alive."

Hu-ung found out a long time ago that her husband Yong-jin was alive in North Korea. Cousins living in Yanbian, China, had told her that Yong-jin had remarried in North Korea and had several children, but she never dreamed that she would see him again.

But she did get to see him at the tourist resort at Mountain Kumgang in North Korea in February 2003, as part of a reunion for people whose families were torn apart by the Korean War. Yong-jin's family, it turns out, had applied for the meeting. They were reunited after 54 years apart, but it ended all too quickly. During the three days at the resort, they were only allowed to be together for five hours.

A few months after the reunion, Hu-ung received a letter from her husband by way of Japan. Yong-jin's letter began with the words "to my beloved wife Kim Hu-ung." She received two more loving letters after that. The bitterness in Kim's heart was washed away when her husband called her "dear" and "honey" and told her that he loved her.

American Navy are dispatched from San Diego to Korea to stop the North Korean invasion.

Unlike the family in the picture, Hu-ung only stole glimpses of her long last husband during the reunion.

2

Chapter Two

THE FOUR RITUALS THAT GIVE PEOPLE LIVES OF DIGNITY

The lifestyle of the *jongga* is rooted in Confucian culture, which places a high priority on ritual propriety (*ye*) as it is called in Korean. Ritual propriety represents a concern for such altruistic pursuits as treating others with courtesy and performing the proper rituals. One lesson that we can learn from the *jongga* is that courtesy and respect are necessary if neighbors and members of society are to trust each, and that these values must be taught in the home.

The Courteous People of the East

In *Treatise on the Dongyi*, a text written by Kong Bin in 268 C.E. during the Han Dynasty of China, ancient Korea is described as "the courteous land in the East":

> The nation is large, but not haughty; its armies are strong, but it does not invade other lands. Because of the gentle customs there,

> people make way for each other on the road, and they allow others to eat before themselves. The men and women of the land live separately and do not mingle together. Surely this is the courteous land in the East!

Since long ago, Korean *seonbi* have been proud of this passage, since it reflects the great respect they had for ritual propriety. In its simplest form, the concept is related to benevolence (*in*), an ideal Confucius defined as "humanness," or people fulfilling their human potential. It is an attribute that demands the control of selfish impulses, as well as putting the needs of others before one's own.

Rituals to Fill One's Human Potential

As an homage to this legacy of ritual propriety, rites of passage can be understood as an expression of courtesy that is centered on the family. Of the variety of rituals that exist in Korea to celebrate life

Members of *jongga* prostrate before a shrine during an ancestral rite. The attendees of a ancetral rite must avoid wearing colored clothing.

events, four are regarded as being particularly important: *gwanrye* (coming-of-age ceremony), *honrye* (traditional wedding), *sangrye* (traditional funeral), and *jerye* (ancestral rites). These rituals are a way for family members to communicate with each other and to affirm their presence, roles, and responsibilities in the family. Along with celebrating family members' development as individuals and marking the milestones along the way, these rituals served as a way to remain in contact with society—both the immediate family and the larger clan. The emphasis that these families' placed on life's continuation by performing these ceremonies at every major life event is likely what brought world-famous anthropologist Claude Lévi-Strauss to Andong.

The roots of these rituals go deep—some all the way back to the time of Dangun, thousands of years ago—and they were further developed when the book *Zhu Xi's Family Rituals* was embraced during the Joseon Dynasty. Aristocrat and commoner alike, Koreans have greeted each turning point in life with the proper ritual, as their circumstances permitted. Though would be impossible to touch upon all each ceremony's intricacies and family-specific interpretations, I hope that a description of my visits to some of the houses where these traditions are preserved today will help readers understand the significance of these rituals.

Gwanrye, Coming-of-Age Ceremony: First of the Four Rituals

Though many of Korea's traditional rites of passage are still performed in some form in the present day, few traces remain of *gwanrye*, the ceremony for those on the cusp of adulthood or who were about to get married. This was the ceremony when men first tied their hair into the topknot and women first pulled their hair into a bun, representing their transition to adulthood.

Gwanrye of Yeongcheon Yi Clan: a boy would finally wear his long braid in a topknot and hence be regarded as a man.

HYEONPUNG GWAK CLAN, GWAK BANG-AN JONGGA: BEING RECOGNIZED AS AN ADULT BEFORE FAMILY AND ANCESTORS

Some *jongga*, however, still perform the traditional *gwanrye* ceremony according to the old customs. One such family is that of Gwak Bang-an (in Sollye Village, Hyeonpung-myeon, Dalseong-gun County, Gyeongsangbuk-do), a *jongga* that is renowned in Korea for its virtue. In April 2002, the coming-of-age ritual was held for Jae-myeong, the 19th descendent of Gwak Bang-an, a government official who was officially recognized for his integrity in the Joseon Dynasty. The *chajongson*, or the eldest son of the surviving *jongson* is joining an impressive family legacy; the government has had monuments built for 12 members of the family, each being extolled

Gwanrye of Jae-myeong, the *chajongson* of Hyeonpung Gwak clan. He is wearing the light green robe that men are given when they pass the civil service exam. It is one of the three robes worn at *gwanrye* that symbolizes different duties of a *seonbi*.

for service as loyal ministers, dutiful sons, and faithful wives.

Jae-myeong's grandmother Kim Du-gyo conveyed the importance of the ritual:

> A long time ago, people would have their *gwanrye* a few days before they got married. At the groom's house, the ritual was more important than the wedding itself. Since we are holding this coming-of-age ceremony for our heir, we will be able to meet our ancestors in the afterlife without shame.

Gwanrye is the first of four major rituals that people must complete as they go through their lives, the reason being that Koreans could not get married until they had assumed the responsibilities of adulthood, a process that this ritual symbolized. In traditional society, *gwanrye* was the first time that men wore the *gat*, a horsehair hat. A 20-year-old man wearing the *gat* was treated as an adult even if he was not married. In fact, men wearing the *gat* could use the informal speech style with those not wearing it, no matter how old they were.

Practicing Adulthood at Gwanrye

An older member of the clan was invited to conduct the ceremony and to read the order of service, which was performed according to the rules laid out in the family's book of etiquette and the customs. During the ritual, Jae-myeong changed out of the clothing of a boy and put on in turn three different adult robes and three different kinds of headwear (as worn during the Joseon Dynasty), one after the other. The officiant shared a word of wisdom with each hat change before arranging Jae-myeong's hair into the adult style: a topknot with specific headgear to hold it in place.

After this, an older member of the family usually gives the person undergoing the ritual some alcohol to drink, but in this case, Jae-myeong drank tea instead. The next stage of the ceremony was when Jae-myeong received his '*ja*,' or second name. In the past, it was considered inappropriate to call someone by the name that their parents had given them, so they were given this additional name upon becoming an adult. This new name is bestowed by the officiant of the ceremony, and Jae-myeong was given the name Su-bong.

After the ritual was over, Jae-myeong's father took Jae-myeong to the family shrine, where, having set up a simple ritual table, he announced to the family ancestors that the family heir had become an adult. This was when Jae-myeong finally bowed to his parents and the other guests, since he had at last assumed the responsibilities of an adult. This was a powerful reminder that *gwanrye* is the first of the four rituals that give people lives of dignity. Once the ritual was over, Jae-myeong said that he had only participated in the ritual because the elders of the family had told him to, but that over the course of the ritual, he had come to a better understanding of the significance of his role as heir to the family line.

Gyobaerye is the part of marriage ceremony where bride and groom are presented to each other for the first time and bow in turn.

Honrye, Traditional Wedding Ceremony: A Life Event to Be Treasured

> *Honrye* brings together two families. It is an opportunity to serve the ancestors who have gone before and the descendants who will come after.

This passage comes from the *Book of Rites*, a Chinese text that is more than 2,000 years old. While *gwanrye* was considered the first of the traditional rituals, it was not as complicated a process as marriage, which constitutes the union of two families. No event in one's life could be more momentous than marriage.

The Meaning of Marriage in a Confucian Society

Traditionally, a marriage was not supposed to favor one party more than the other; rather, it was thought signify the harmonious conjunction of yin and yang, the reason why most ceremonies were held at sunset—when yin (light) and yang (dark) meet. This relationship is aptly illustrated by the fact that the Chinese character for marriage (婚) contains the Chinese character for sunset (昏).

It is important to understand the concept of yin and yang to appreciate a *honrye*. Yin and yang are opposing powers appear contradictory but are actually interdependent, like shadow and light. This worldview characterized female as yin and male as yang, and in a *honrye*, the two met to become whole and give rise to each other. Many details of the ceremony ascribe to the concept, wishing the young couple harmony and reproduction. Continuing the family line was one of the greatest duty of any person, and harmony of yin and yang was also understood as what gave rise to life.

Naju Yim Clan, Yim Tak Jongga: Wedding Day for the Heir to a Family Going Back 600 Years

Though the parents of a *jongga* heir would typically prefer a traditional wedding, the event will often take place in a contemporary hall to satisfy both families. However, the *honrye* for Yim Jeong-yeol, *jongson* to the Naju Yim Clan in Dasi-myeon, Naju, Jeollanam-do, was held in the front yard at the family house—a request from his fiancée, much to Yim's

Jokduri, an elaborate headdress all brides must don. In *jongga*, it was often handed down for generations and mother-in-law would often send it to the bride-to-be.

mother's happy surprise.

The ceremonial table set up in the yard in front of the women's quarters held a pair of candles, along with dishes containing sorghum, soybeans, millet, and red beans. There was a plate filled with cottonseeds and other dishes holding chestnuts, dates, and persimmons. The grains are said to symbolize wealth; the cottonseeds, clothing; and the chestnuts, dates, and persimmons, long life and many children. The abundance of the table was augmented by beautiful flowers in a pair of vases. A hen and rooster, standing in for the mythical phoenix, were face to face, with their legs tied together. The table also held blue and red thread, a pair of gourds, and two drinking glasses. No cooked food was on the table, however, perhaps because it was only ceremonial.

The Many Stages of Honrye

The bride arrived first riding on a colorful palanquin and was waiting in the women's quarters. The groom rode up on a black horse and got off in front of the gate. He looked splendid in a regal black hat and the formal robes that his ancestors had once worn in the royal court. As he stepped through the gate into the estate, he partially covered his face with a small roll of paper known as a *chemyeon*. The custom of covering the face is said to originate from the natural bashfulness that people feel when they are the center of attention.

Before the main part of the ceremony was a ritual called *jeonanrye*, in which the groom placed a pair of wooden geese on the ceremonial table and then bowed. Geese are known for never changing partners, and they represent the groom's wish for a happy life, as well as a vow to never leave his wife as long as he lives.

After this, the groom entered the main area and stood on the east side of the ceremonial table. The East symbolizes man, since that is where the sun rises; the West represents woman, since that is where it sets. This is again derived from the traditional philosophy of yin yang, which sees East as yang and West as yin.

At last, the beautiful bride appeared on the arms of several helpers. She was wearing the traditional headpiece and dress, her hands concealed by elegant white cloth covers. The bride and groom stood and faced each other, and then got down on their knees. Helpers assisted them with a hand-washing ritual, since the bride and groom's body and mind are to be clean before they begin the sacred ceremony of marriage.

Next, the bride and groom greeted each other formally, the bride bowing to the groom, and the groom to the bride. The groom stood while the bride bowed to him, while the bride sat down to receive her bow. This is another gesture that emphasizes the different nature and role of male and female in a Confucian society.

In the next stage of the ceremony, the bride and groom drink alcohol from glasses and two gourd dippers. Before taking a drink, they pour a little on the ground three times, symbolizing that they are making their marriage vows before the gods of heaven and earth. The drink of alcohol that they share signifies their conjugal bond. The two dippers are made from the two halves of a single gourd. These two halves are

In the Joseon Dynasty, the bride would rarely show her face, keep her head down the entire time and rely on her aids to guide her through the ritual. This was to appear bashful and modest.

Pyebaek food also carries meaning. Beef jerky in the far right is shaped like a wide plain, in hopes that the mother-in-law will accept the daughter-in-law with such a wide heart. Dates symbolizes many children because date trees yield fruit for every flower.

unique in the world; when they come together, they form a perfect whole, just like a man and woman when they marry.

Pyebaek: Becoming a Part of the Groom's Family

A different wedding table is set and then the bride performed *pyebaek*, the ritual in which the new wife formally bows to her parents-in-law for the first time. Traditionally, the *honrye* would take place at the bride's house, and *pyeback* was held when the couple returns to the groom's house, but since this wedding ceremony was already taking place at the groom's house, the *pyeback* took place on that day.

The food that the bride had prepared to offer her mother-in-law as part of the ceremony included beef jerky, dates, chestnuts, *gujeolpan* (an elaborate dish made of nine separate ingredients), and alcohol. The bride made four low bows before her mother-in-law, after which point the elder woman tossed some dates into the folds of the bride's skirt, symbolizing the hope that the bride would bear a son. After that, the bride bowed to the rest of her in-laws, according to their generational rank and how closely they were related to the groom.

The wedding robes that the bride and groom were wearing were family heirlooms, worn by the groom's own parents when they were married. The groom's formal robes was likely one inherited from many family members who had served in high offices during the *jongga's* 600-year history. Brides also wore the same headpiece, a *jokduri* that their mother-in-law wore for both the wedding ceremony and *pyebaek*.

Sangrye, Traditional Funeral: Saying Goodbye to Parents Whose Duty Is Done

The third of the rituals is *sangrye*, or the traditional funeral, when family members bade their final farewell. This was a complicated ritual that was not done until the family had completed the period of mourning. The ritual was an opportunity to express gratitude to your parents for raising you and to reflect on where you came from.

The *sangju* (eldest son or closest male relative of the deceased) shows grief

Andong Kim Clan, Kim Seok-gyu Jongga: the Funeral Rite of a 98-year-old Jongbu

Yi Jong-gyu's life as a *jongbu* began the day she married into a *jongga* descended from Kim Seok-gyu, a scholar at the end of the Joseon Dynasty whose house was is in Docheon-ri, Myeongho-myeon, Bonghwa-gun, Gyeongsangbuk-do. Yi dedicated herself to the household for nearly three quarters of a century and you could see the respect with which she was regarded in the traditional funeral ceremony that took place on a cold February day. Big flakes of snow drifted down and a somber mood dispersed among mourners.

At the wake, which was held on the porch of the family home, there was a ritual chair, its small seat propped up high on long legs. In front of it was a cloth spread out to sit under the ritual table, followed by another table for incense. A bowl of drink was placed in front of the incense table, with a photograph of the deceased and a temporary memorial tablet on the chair. The mourners wore white robes and traditional head coverings, which were high, quadrangular-shaped hemp hat.

The Long Sendoff for Grandmother

On the morning of the third day of the wake was the *barinje*, a ceremony where the deceased is offered a final ceremonial meal and the surviving relatives bid them goodbye. At the beginning of the rite, the officiant held up a glass of alcohol and then knelt to read a prayer to the deceased: "We have prepared a funeral bier to take you to the grave. Having completed the rites for your departure, we now bid you farewell forever." All of Yi's mourners wept and bowed, and after the pallbearers were fed a meal, the group prepared to depart for the burial site, a ritual known as *chulsang*.

The procession was led by black funereal flags, along with a red banner announcing the deceased and a hempen cloth that would be used later to wipe down the coffin before lowering it into the grave. These were followed by Yi's 19-year-old great-grandson Do-nyeon, who carried an elegant photograph of his grandmother. After him came the funeral bier, supported by 18 bearers. After the bier passed, around 40 men who were direct descendants of the deceased came next, as well as other mourners. Since women are not permitted to accompany the bier to the gravesite, they saw the group off outside the entrance to the village, lamenting as the bearers sang a sad song of mourning.

Traditional Burial Process

Yi's burial plot was on a low hill about two kilometers from the house. A hole had already been dug in the ground large enough to hold the coffin. When the bier arrived, a simple offering was prepared in front of the temporary memorial tablet, and the mourners who had come to the gravesite said their condolences to the bereaved. The hempen cloth was then used to wipe down the coffin, which was finally lowered into the grave. Next, after the geomancer confirmed the proper orientation with a ritual compass, the red banner was neatly arranged upon the coffin. At this point, the bereaved family members bowed twice and wept as they covered the coffin with dirt. Once the grave was filled, the bier, which had since been disassembled, was burned. *Chulsang* was finished when the family members returned to the house carrying the memorial tablet.

For a funeral procession of a well respected elder, the whole town would follow.

Traditionally speaking, *sangrye* involves a number of other rituals that are to be held during the three years after *chulsang*, and the family is to remain in mourning for those three years. It is only after mourning is complete that the family installs the permanent memorial tablet in the family shrine and begins holding the ancestral rites on the anniversary of the departed's death and Korea's two major festivals, Seollal (the Lunar New Year) and Chuseok (the Autumn Harvest Festival).

An incense burner is essential to most ancestral rites

Jerye, Ancestral Rites: Lifelong Responsibility of the Family Head

The most distinctive and relatively well preserved of Korea's four traditional rituals is *jerye*. The term covers a spectrum of ancestral rites performed in honor of departed ancestors. This includes the nation's royal ancestors, some of whose memorial tablets are housed at the UNESCO-sanctioned Jongmyo Shrine in Seoul, a site where the government holds ancestral rites each year. But Jongmyo is not the only place such a shrine can be found; shrines are also maintained by traditional Korean families scattered around the country. The longstanding importance of these family shrines is suggested by their close proximity to the family home. The reverence shown is perhaps not surprising, given that Korean ancestral rites have been in practice on the

Korean peninsula in some form or another for 2,000 years, from Three Kingdoms Period to this day.

Ancestral Rites and their Significance

The process of showing honor to the ancestors whose memorial tablets are stored in the family shrine requires appropriate attire and the careful preparation of a large number of ceremonial dishes and donning. Most families conduct 30 such rituals in a single year, with some families performing more than 50. One benefit of the ancestral rites is that, after the ceremony is over, families share the food with their neighbors. During times of poverty, this food not only kept the Korean people healthy but also had a significant influence on the development of culinary culture on the peninsula.

These ceremonial rituals, which are performed by many Korean families, serve a dual purpose: They connect family members to the past, while also giving them an opportunity to reunite and reaffirm their shared heritage. It was these ancestral rites that preserved the foundation of traditional Korean culture and ensured the survival of the unique family bonds that developed during the Joseon Dynasty.

Ancestral rites connect family members to the past, while also giving them an opportunity to reunite and reaffirm their shared heritage

Jongga, the Staunch Observers of Ancestral Rites

The importance of the ancestral rites can also be seen in the heads of the *jongga*, who remain dedicated to their responsibility to carry on the family line and hold rituals honoring their ancestors. It isn't difficult to see how these two tasks are intrinsically linked, as extending the family line is still paramount to ensuring that the rituals will continue tobe observed by the next generation. In some cases, this responsibility has supplanted the family head's other career aspirations, at least in the usual sense. In addition to managing family affairs and performing the ancestral rites, those hoping to live up to clan expectations must commit to hosting a steady stream of visitors to the family home and be well-versed in the family history.

This genealogical knowledge goes beyond the names and generational order of their ancestors. Family heads are expected to know their ancestors' ranks in the civil service and their major accomplishments. To be respected as heir of the family line, they

For ancestral rites, *seonbi* wore smocks of hemp cloth which represents frugality and sorrow. It's an ancient tradition that comes from Maui Taeja (The crown prince in hemp smock), the last crown prince of Silla (57 B.C.–A.D.935), who wore hemp cloth in mourning for his country.

must know the lifestyle of their ancestors and anecdotes from their lives. They should also know when ancestral rites are to be performed for their direct ancestors and where they were buried. Many of these family heirs are taught to read ancient texts and are trained to do calligraphy. Finally, they are expected toknow the names, familial relationships, and dates of ancestral rites for their close relatives so that they could honor them with a visit at the right times. Needless to say, the heirs must be able to finance all of these activities.

Different Types of Ancestral Rites

What follows are just a few of the ancestral rites that *jongga* are responsible for performing. The most basic are the rituals held on the anniversary of ancestors' death, called *gije*; the rituals held on the morning of the Seollal (the Lunar New Year) and the Chuseok (the Autumn Harvest Festival), called *charye*; and rituals performed in front of the grave, called *myoje*. The general rule was that ancestral rites were only performed for four generations of ancestors. However, in the case of an ancestor who had performed distinguished service for the country or for the family, an exception was granted, known as *bulcheonwi*, which allowed the family to perform the rites for this person forever. In the city of Andong in Gyeongsangbuk-do, where Confucian culture is still held in high esteem, only families performing this last kind of ritual are regarded as *jongga* in the strictest sense of the word.

A *seonbi* is shaving chestnuts in preparation for *jesa*, or ancestral rite. He wears the mask to prevent spit from getting into the food for purity was important. In some *jongga* the whole process of ancestral rites involved only the members of the household.

Jangsu Hwang Clan, Hwang hui Jongga: Bulcheonwi Rite for Hwang Hui, Paragon of the Honest Official

Hwang Hui was a state councilor in the early part of the Joseon Dynasty, but he is still renowned today for his integrity and consummate statesmanship as a public servant. As such, it was only natural that his descendants would be granted the right to offer ancestral rites to him perpetually. The *bulcheonwi* rite for this significant ancestor was held at the shrine where his spirit tablet is housed, in Geumseong-ri, Tanhyeon-myeon, Paju, Gyeonggi-do.

On February 7 of each year according to the lunar calendar, members of the clan gather from around the country—Gyeongsangbuk-do, Daejeon, Seoul, and beyond—to hold ancestral rites for this great man. A variety of family members are chosen to perform important parts of the ritual, one of which being that a glass of alcohol is to be lifted three times, each time by a different family member. Another person reads the order of the ritual, and still another reads a prayer to the departed.

Bangujeong is the pavilion where Hwang Hui spent his years after retirement at age 86. The name literally means a place where you enjoy nature in company of seagulls.

Left: Hwang Hui's portrait
Right: Scene of Hwang Hui's *bulcheonwi*, held at a shrine next to Bangujeong

Respecting the Words of Forefathers

The ritual was scheduled to start early in the morning of February 8 by the lunar calendar, the date of Hwang Hui's death. At 10 o'clock the previous evening, the food was arranged on the ritual table in the family shrine.

The ancestral rite was conducted according to the ancient customs of the family and, aside from ritual hand-washing for the participants, it closely resembled other standard ancestral rites. Many families take pride in making the *bulcheonwi* ritual a splendid affair, but the ceremony for Hwang Hui was simple, while still retaining an appropriate degree of solemnity. This was to respect Hwang Hui's last words, which were a request to his family to perform the funeral and ancestral rites according to *Zhu Xi's Family Rituals* without any unnecessary pretense or show.

Saving the Only Heir of the Six Martyred Ministers

The Jongga of Bak Paeng-nyeon from the Suncheon Bak clan.

When King Sejo, uncle of King Danjong, deposed his young nephew and usurped the throne, six figures masterminded an abortive coup to restore the rightful king. These figures, today known as the six martyred ministers, were Seong Sam-mun, Bak Paeng-nyeon, Ha Wi-ji, Yi Gae, Yu Eung-bu, and Yu Seong-won. Since they and their entirely families were slaughtered for their treason, it is no surprise that none of their direct descendants survive today. Well, except for Bak Paeng-nyeon, that is. Thanks to the quick thinking of Bak's daughter-in-law, who was pregnant with his grandson when disaster befell on the family, that line still survives 550 years later, and it is now in its 20th generation.

When Bak was accused of treason, his punishment extended to his entire family. His father, brothers, and sons were put to death, and his wives were sold as slaves or became slaves of the government. His son's second wife, a member of the Seongju Yi clan, became a government slave, but as luck would have it she was assigned to Daegu, where her father Yi Cheol-geun was mayor.

At this time, Bak's daughter-in-law Yi was pregnant. According to royal decree, if she bore a son, it would be killed, and if she bore a daughter, it would become a government slave. Late in the autumn of that year, she at last gave birth: it was a boy. She knew that the royal decree could not be defied: if she told the authorities about her son, he would be killed, and Bak's family line would be extinguished forever. But providentially, a female servant in her family's house gave birth to a daughter around the same time. That was when Yi had her inspiration.

"If we swap our children, my boy's life will be saved!" she thought. This quick thinking enabled the grandson of the disgraced government official Bak Paeng-nyeon to survive under the name of Bak Bi, since everyone thought he was the son of a slave in the mayor's household.

Until the age of 17, Bak Bi was raised as the son of a slave, concealing his true identity. In the third year of the reign of King Seongjong, Yi Geuk-gyun, who had been appointed governor of Gyeongsang Province, visited the house of his wife's family in Myotgol. Yi Geuk-gyun was in fact Bak Bi's uncle—he was married to the sister of Bak Bi's mother Yi—and on this visit he learned what had happened. Yi Geuk-gyun wept upon hearing the remarkable story. He

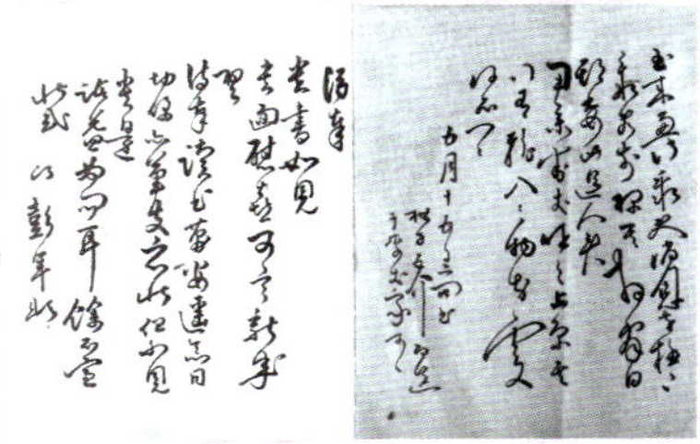

Letters between Seong Sam-mun and Bak Paeng-nyeon who were close friends

Ancestral rite is held to honor the six martyrs and their royalty

advised Bak Bi, now a grown man, to turn himself in. Sejo had died some time before, he pointed out, and Sejo's grandson Seongjong was now on the throne.

When King Seongjong heard Bak Bi's confession, he was deeply moved. The King gave Bak Bi the name Ilsan, meaning the one precious stone left behind by the six martyred ministers, and freed him as well, needless to say. This is how Bak Il-san, grandson of Bak Paeng-nyeon, became the founder of the Chungjeonggong branch of the family.

The sacrifices that Bak Paeng-nyeon's descendents have made to carry on their illustrious ancestor's family name are impressive. The *jongga* is currently being taken care of by Bak Jong-deok, the third son. When Jong-jin, his eldest brother and the 19th heir to the family line, passed away at the age of 55, Jong-deok wrapped up his affairs in Seoul and took up residence at the *jongga*. But before this, Jong-deok had already sent his only son Wan-sun to become the adopted son of his eldest brother, to ensure, in other words, that he had an heir. This involved filling out a death certificate for his son and then reporting his birth once again under his brother's name.

I asked Wan-sun's birth mother, whose family name is Kwon, how it felt to give up her only son for adoption. She said she didn't think much of it while he was at home, but then he went to school

> It really hurt me every time teachers who didn't know the whole story would ask me why the child didn't have any parents. But there was nothing to be done. We couldn't just let the family line of the *jongga* die out, could we?

3

Chapter Three

FOOD CULTURE OF THE JONGGA: FROM THE MOUTH TO THE HEART

Until fairly recently, it was difficult for most people to experience the food served at a Korean *jongga* first-hand. The meals prepared in these houses represented both the dignity and wealth of the family, as well as the culinary talent of its matriarch; the quality was so revealing that many *jongga* were unwilling to be interviewed in matters concerning food.

Still, I thought it would be a shame if Koreans allowed this precious culinary and cultural heritage, complete with its own historical development and scientific techniques, to go to waste without anyone at least attempting to document its nuances. This motivated me to persuade a few of these families to give me access to the culinary traditions that they had been guarding so jealously. Over the course of 20 years, I visited the kitchens in the women's quarters of over two hundred *jongga*, sampling nearly four thousand different dishes.

The Role and Significance of Food in Jongga

The food of the *jongga* includes dishes prepared for rites of passage held at key moments in the lives of family members, such as weddings and funerals, as well as seasonal dishes designed to take advantage of the ingredients available during Korea's four seasons. These families are also expected to prepare unique and pleasing dishes to entertain family members and others who pay a visit. Indeed, the food prepared for guests is the most important of all, as it intimates the wealth of the family while also testing the culinary prowess of the lady of the house. This wife's skill also determines the flavor of the various fermented foods that serve as the foundation of Korean cuisine: soybean paste, red pepper paste, soy sauce, and alcohol.

Jongga's food prepared for guests. Notice how the utensils have been set horizontally rather than vertically, with ends slightly protruding from the edge of the table.

In the adept hands of the family matron, with her extensive knowledge of the region, a single ingredient could blossom into dozens of different and delicious flavors. Take, for example,the families I visited in Pohang, Gyeongsangbuk-do, and Seoji Village in Gangneung, Gangwon-do, seaside areas with an abundance of fish. The wives of these families concocted countless unique dishes using the same fish, whether it was diced and served raw, grilled over charcoal, wrapped in bamboo leaves or pine needles to remove any odor and then boiled, deep-fried in oil, left to simmer in a thick soup, tossed in a stew, or dried and seasoned with *gochujang* and served as a side dish. These women's knack for taking a variety of approaches to the same ingredients was indicative of each family's deep roots in the region.

The food of the *jongga* also functioned as a means of promoting harmony in the immediate family, among friends and relatives, with neighbors, and in the village. The dishes prepared in these homes are instilled with the collective spirit inherited from the farmers of

the past who realized that they could finish their work more quickly when they helped one another. Some families have cookbooks that are more than 350 years old, such as *Eumsik Dimibang* (How to Learn the Taste of Food), which is said to be the first cookbook in Asia written by a woman. Such books hint at the long history of these dishes. A *jongson* of one family said that he is living exactly as his ancestors lived for the past thousand years, underlining the fact that the food of these families has changed little over the years.

Jongga Food and Cultural Heritage

At the *jongga*, preserving the dishes served at that home is what anchors the preservation of the home's overall lifestyle. Each of these dishes has its own culture—rules, tools, and concepts—that help give Korean cuisine its distinctive identity. By definition, the *jongga* is a place where the ancestral rites are performed and where visitors are shown hospitality. The person with the grave responsibility of spearheading the home's rituals and hospitality—namely, making the dozens of dishes that are needed for each—is the woman of this house, the wife of the family heir.

Jongbu helped preserve *jongga's* distinctive identity through food.

The women I met at the *jongga* take great pride in their work and great pleasure in the fact that they are preserving Korean customs and traditions. One elderly woman told me with confidence in her voice that, if she had to do it all over again, she would choose the same life.

Miryang Son Clan, Son Seong-jeung Jongga: Delicacies of the Richest Jongga in Gyeongsangnam-do

At Gyodong Village in Miryang, a city renowned for its rendition of the folk tune "Arirang" and for the Yeongnamru Pavilion, you can visit a 99-*kan* house that preserves its authenticity despite its great age. This home has been lived in by12 generations of descendants of Son Seong-jeung (1700–1756; pen name: Inmukjae), who was renowned for academic accomplishment and filial piety in the time of King Sukjong (r. 1674–1720).

Gujeolpan is a popular dish also known as royal cuisine.

The family that was once the wealthiest in all of Gyeonsangnam-do managed to hold on to their ancestral home despite various twists of fortune, and even today it continues the formal practice of serving elaborate meals with seven side dishes. This family has also opened up the house to visitors to show them what the food of the *jongga* is really like. Now anyone can experience the authentic Korean food of the *jongga*, a style that is being forgotten today, in the men's quarters of this genteel house. The woman of the house briefed me about the various kinds of meals that she prepares.

Different Meals for Different Occasions

The food served in the Son Seong-jung house varies with the number of side dishes on the table, and there are a number of other traditions that are also observed (note: side dishes exclude rice, soup, stew, kimchi, and sauce). One such example is that family members are typically given three side dishes at breakfast and five at dinner, but guests are always served seven. Meals are also prepared differently when served to one person than when served to two, and when villagers labor together on the farm, they sit on the ground to eat a communal meal with portions for three or more people. The main starch served with these meals can be rice, porridge, or noodles, and there are also dishes served along with alcohol. The family has special recipes for the dishes that must be prepared for various ceremonies, such as the food served on the *dol*, a baby's first birthday; the wedding feast; the food and alcohol served for one's parents on their birthdays; and the ritual food used in ancestral rites.

Serving Guests with Their Best

The family used luxurious, heavy brass tableware when serving visitors. They own several sets of these, since brass keeps the food warm in the winter and is also healthier for the body. For my meal,

When serving guests, all the lids of the dishes are closed to keep the food warm and clean. Should there be a letter on the lids,they are positioned so the guest can read it.

The seven side dish meal for guests prepared by Miryang Son Clan's *jongbu*.

which was a typical meal for guests of seven side dishes, a total of 15 tablewares were brought to the table. They were different in size, and each of them contained rare delicacies.

The various dishes were carried out with their lid on to keep the food warm, and arranged so that the writing on the lid would face the person eating. The utensils were placed on the right, with the spoon in front and the chopsticks behind. They were positioned on the edge of the table so that they would protrude about 2cm over the edge of the table.

The dishes also had to be laid out in a certain order on the table. In the first row (closest to the person eating) were rice, vegetables, and soup, from left to right. The stew was placed behind the soup, with the soy sauce between them. The vinegar soy sauce was on the right, and the vinegar red pepper sauce was on the left. Warm foods like grilled meat and boiled fish were on the right, while cold food, including dried abalone, strips of boiled meat, and beef tartar were on the left. Vegetables, both boiled and raw, were included in the row of fish and meat pancakes, while the dry side dishes and the salted seafood were placed in the row of side dishes on the left. The kimchi appeared on the row at the very back of the table, with cabbage kimchi, a soup made of eggs and octopus called *suranchaeguk*, and white kimchi arranged from left to right.

Unique Home-brew

Most *jongga* brewed their own liquor and Sons were no exception. The Son Seong-jeung family had a special homebrewed alcohol that they served to visitors to the village. The alcohol, which is made by mixing sticky rice with a fermentation starter called *nuruk*, is brewed before gatherings at the house, ancestral rites, or the arrival of an important visitor. The drink has a number of nicknames, sometimes called "golden brew" because of its color, and also "20-day brew" because of the time it takes to ferment. The snack served to accompany the drink is made of ground-up beef jerky, flakes of dried pollack, and boiled egg yolk, which is kneaded together with honey and sesame seed oil and then placed in a cookie tray. The end result is a snack that presents beautifully and is also very convenient to serve at large gatherings.

The process of brewing *makgeoli*, a traditional drink.

Top: the view looks out to Yun Jeung Jongga and its field of fermenting soy sauce pots. The *jongga's* famous soy sauce is made through a very elaborate process that relies on high quality ingredients and the expertise of *jongbu*.

Right: In much of Korean food like *bulgogi*, good soy sauce is the key ingredient.

Bottom: *Tteokseon*, the dish the Yun Jeung Jongga invented that won the *jongga* food competition.

Papyeong Yun Clan, Yun Jeung Jongga: First Prize in a National Jongga Food Competition

Ritual food is an elaborate affair, but this family has kept it so simple that they didn't even put rice cake on the table for the ancestral rites. This is the family of Yun Jeung (1629–1714; pen name: Myeongjae), from the Nojong branch of the Papyeong Yun Clan, the clan from which more queens came than any other clan during the Joseon Dynasty.

Considerate Words of a Loving Ancestor

Yun Jeung was a scholar and head of the Soron (new learning) faction during the time of King Sukjong. Observing the bickering between Soron and its rival faction Noron (old learning), Yun eventually came to despise power. He resigned his government position and returned home, where he dedicated his time to teaching the next generation of students. The simplicity of their ancestral rite food was because they observed Yun Jeung's instructions that were rooted in his love for his family. Worried that his descendants might run into financial difficulties and have trouble preparing all of the food that the rites usually demand, Yun Jeung instructed them not to waste rice cake by putting it on the ritual table. He also told them not to prepare *yumilgwa*, a type of cookie, because of the time required to make it, or pancakes, since these required oil.

However, their frugality does not mean the *jongga's* food is plain. The family's soy sauce is made through an intensely laborious process that takes approximately a year to produce and mature. Yet it is known to be worth the effort: the soy sauce tastes so good that family members call the soy sauce pot the "honey pot." In Korean food, it's often the sauce that's the key to taste.

Perhaps due to its soy sauce, Yun Jeung *jongga* won the first prize in a 1998 culinary competition between numerous *jongga* around Korea famous for their food. The dish submitted to the competition was a royal rice cake concoction called *tteokseon*, which featured her homemade soy sauce. The dish is made by seasoning rice cake bars, finely ground beef, *seogi* mushrooms, and eggs with soy sauce. The rice cake bars are chopped into 5cm segments and then split in half. Next, horizontal notches are cut into the rice cake, with the knife held at an angle, and these notches are stuffed with strips of stir-fried beef, mushrooms, egg yolk, and egg whites. The stuffed halves of rice cake are then steamed slightly. They are to be dipped in soy sauce and eaten while hot. The dish is a colorful addition to the food prepared for guests at the New Year.

Gyeongju Yi Clan, Yi Hang-bok Jongga : Soybean Paste Passed Down for Five Hundred Years

Portrait of Yi Hang-bok, who served as high government official, is famous for his wit and loyalty.

The family home of Yi Hang-bok (1556–1618; pen name: Baeksa), regarded as one of the four greatest public officials during the Joseon Dynasty, is located at Geumhyeon-ri, Gasan-myeon, Pocheon, Gyeonggi-do. When I visited the family home of Yi Hang-bok one November day, there were around 100 large pots in the storage area for condiments such as soy sauce, soybean paste, and red pepper paste, which are still made according to recipes passed down from generation to generation. You could tell how busy this *jongga* must be during the time of the year.

Food Preparations of Jongga for Winter

In autumn, after the harvest is over, *jongga* people must work even harder than usual as they prepare for winter rituals and food. Various rituals that take place during these months; one such ceremony is held at the shrine to inform the ancestors that the harvest has been brought in; another is offered to the household gods to express gratitude for the year's harvest. Then families proceed to make kimchi, but the work is far from done. It is now time to boil the soybeans to make *meju*, an important ingredient used for making soy sauce, soybean paste, and other fermented condiments. After hanging the *meju* up to dry, the family barely has a chance to relax before it's time for the ritual held on *dongji*, the winter solstice.

The first step to making good soybean paste is boiling soybeans in an old fashioned iron pot over a fire fueled with wood.

Working to Preserve Traditional Flavor

I was permitted to visit the *jongga* on the day that they were boiling the soybeans for the *meju*. From which all the pots will be filled again eventually. The day doubles

Meju, made of crushed boiled soybeans, is fermented indoors during the winter and then hung out to dry in early spring. Afterwards, *meju* is soaked in salt water and fermented some more until it is finally made into soybean paste.

as a party for the entire neighborhood, giving me a rare opportunity to experience the autumnal abundance of the *jongga*. There I met Yi Sang-uk, the 14th heir in the line of Yi Hang-bok, and his wife, Jo Byeong-hui. Yi said he had studied engineering at Hanyang University and had worked as an architect and rancher, but he looked more like a noble scholar of old. His wife Jo, born in the Pungyang Jo Clan, married Yi and joined the family at the age of 27. Since then, she has fulfilled all of the responsibilities of wife and mother, bearing and raising two sons and two daughters, as well as preserving family's pastes. As if preparing the food for the ancestral rites sixteen times a year by herself didn't keep her busy enough, Jo was also bravely boiling 50 sacks of soybeans in a huge cauldron. She was working to keep up with demand for the family's legendary paste, a task that most people would never dream of attempting, but one which Jo managed with ease. She was also teaching the next generation the family recipe for pastes, hoping to maintain the flavor that had been

Hwasanseowon, shrine of Yi Hang-bok at Pocheon

preserved for so many years.

The simple lunch meal that Jo prepared for me included a bubbling hot soybean paste stew in an earthenware pot, savory cabbage leaves that were perfect for dipping in red pepper paste, and delicious yellow croaker jerky. The meal appeared to reflect the modest tastes of Yi Hang-bok, who was an official praised by the government for his integrity.

Handing Down Knowledge Instead of Money

Segeoji, the village of Nampyeong Mun Clan, where both Insumungo and Subongjeongsa are located.

Mun Dal-gyu Family (Nampyeong Mun Clan)

Considering how highly reading was regarded in traditional Korean society, it's no surprise that books were treasured. At the time, books were costly and hard to come by, and Korea's *seonbi* valued them nearly as much as life itself. This could certainly be said of the Nampyeong Mun Clan, which established a library called Mangwondang near the family house at Inheung-ri, Daegu, in 1910, for the benefit of their pupils. Today, the building is known as Insumungo. It is the largest collection of books owned by a single Korean family, and it houses more ancient texts than any other private library in the country. There are 20,000 volumes in the library's collection, far larger than the library of any Confucian school. The library has also worked hard to keep the books in good condition. The collection contains around 1,000 valuable books, including a number of extremely rare books that predate the Imjin War. The books are sorted and stored in boxes made of paulownia wood.

When the library was established, transportation was slow and Korea had little contact with the outside world. How in the world was the family able to build such a large collection of books? To begin with, certain friends of the family living in China, Korean historians living in exile there, send books by ship to the port of Mokpo in southwest Korea. At the time, the only way to transport books over land was by oxcart, so carts loaded with hundreds of books would go from Mokpo to Namwon on the slopes of Jirisan Mountain. From Namwon, the carts had to cross the rugged hills of Hamyang and Geochang, finally reaching Mangwondang at the house of the Nampyeong Mun Clan in Inheung-ri, Daegu. Each shipment of the books took several months. This is how the Mangwondang collection was put together, requiring an immense amount of money, time, and effort.

What kind of books can you find at Insumungo? While the library includes books from various genres, history books make up a substantial part of the collection. Partly, this is because of the emphasis that Confucian thinkers placed on reading about and learning from the classics, but it was also because of the crisis on the Korean peninsula. As it happened, the Mangwondang library was established in 1910, the same year that Korea was annexed by Japan. Mangwondang was not only set up to promote the education of the family's children, but also as a self-defense measure, aimed at keeping the Korean spirit from being conquered by the new kinds of education that the Japanese were implementing. To defend the national spirit, there was a need for historical understanding, and for proper education.

In 1910, the Gwanggeodang estate was built and Mangwondang established inside it. The library served as a kind of cultural center, with writers and scholars from around the country visiting to debate learning, the arts, and the future of Korea, and the fame of the Nampyeong Mun Clan began to grow. Numerous people stayed for months at a time to read the books in the collection, and they were provided with writing tools to aid their study. The library could be called the spiritual home of the independence movement.

Establishing Mangwondang required two things: a vast amount of money and an enormous passion for learning. It is likely that the library would never have become a reality without the concerted effort of a father and son from the Nampyeong Mun Clan: Mun Bong-seong and Mun Yeong-bak. Mun Bong-seong, the father, used his financial acumen to fill the family coffers, while Mun Yeong-bak, his second son, applied those vast financial resources to the project of building Mangwondang. Completing this project required not only purchasing books but also printing important Confucian texts.

Even today, scholars continue to visit Insumungo to research Eastern philosophy and the classics. From Mangwondang library, we can infer how highly Koreans of the past valued academic learning and the national spirit.

Paulownia trees are reputed to keep out moisture and insects. The boxes of paulownia wood in the library were all made to order for the purpose of protecting books.

4

Chapter Four

JONGTAEK, THE HOUSE THAT GENERATIONS HAVE CALLED HOME

For people today, who are accustomed to economic growth, rapid change, and the loneliness of individualism, the *jongga* is a beacon shining through the centuries, a symbol of the communal and ethical worldview of traditional society, which sought the meaning of life in human relationships. The best way to encounter the history, traditions, lifestyle, and spirit of the *jongga* is by visiting the *jongga* houses, which are located at beautiful, auspicious locations around Korea. These houses, where the *jongga* have resided for generations, are known as *jongtaek*.

THE CHARACTERISTIC OF A JONGTAEK

Most of these family homes are located in places of natural beauty. Many families selected the site of their house according to the principles of geomancy, or *pungsujiri*. According to this theory, sites of natural beauty possess a mysterious energy, and this inherently natural energy propels the people born at such sites into greatness. Thanks to this placement, a visit to one of these houses is a relaxing experience. It is a time to rest your weary spirit, appreciate the tranquility of the beautiful surroundings and beauty of nature, and absorb the positive energy found there.

Jongtaek, the Place Experience True Family Values

As has already been stated, *jongga* were founded by individuals who had delivered the nation in a time of trouble or whose scholarly achievements had earned them the reputation of being a spiritual teacher for the nation. The descendents of the founder, who inherited both his teachings and his spirit, spent their lives

Nongam Jongtaek is enveloped by mountains. Korean traditional architecture was about becoming a part of nature rather than standing out from it. Location and natural surroundings was regarded with more importance than the building itself, since it was widely believed that an auspicious site will help the family prosper.

living in the house that the founder had built and were the ones responsible for maintaining it. Thus, whether big or small, elaborate or plain, these compounds and all of the buildings in them are characterized by an intimacy with nature, as well as the influence of Confucian philosophy. Nearly all of the houses are made of wood, offering a glimpse into the architectural style used by the upper classes during the Joseon Dynasty.

The members of a *jongga* thought of themselves as a bridge between their ancestors and their descendents, messengers charged with conveying the teachings and ideology of their forebearers to their heirs. As a result, the descendents carefully stored the papers written by illustrious ancestors and letters they had exchanged with other great figures of their time in various places inside the house, to prevent the spiritual teachings of their ancestors from being lost in the event of calamity. For this reason, these houses are also repositories of relics that would be worth immense sums if put on the market today.

Lastly, these homes also house precious artifacts that illustrate, among other things how the family members, who were greatly respected as the leaders of traditional society, carried out their duties and fulfilled their moral and social responsibility through their consideration for others. Best of all is to meet the male head of the family, his wife, and other family members, who have been educated in the ways of their specific family from an early age. The dignity of the *seonbi* and concern for other people are a way of life for such individuals.

Although Korean traditional culture is vanishing amid the rapid pace of industrialization and Westernization, several hundred of these homes still remain in Korea today. In this chapter, I will introduce you to several of Korea's best-known *jongtaek*, spaces where you can experience the aforementioned values for yourself.

Unjoru in spring time

MUNHWA RYU CLAN GONSANGUN JONGGA: UNJORU, ONE OF THE THREE MOST PROPITIOUS SITES IN SOUTH KOREA

"The genius is born of the wind and earth."

The phrase is found in a statistical assessment of the influence of climate and terrain in *The Man of Genius*, a book written by the Italian Cesare Lombroso in the late 19th century. It is similar to the old Korean saying that good people are born near good hills and rivers.

The Meaning and Beauty of Unjoru's Site

Because of the importance that the *seonbi* of old placed on the birth of descendents who would bring glory to the family and ensure its prosperity for generations to come, most of Korea's better-known old family homes are located at sites that are considered favorable according to *pungsujiri*, or geomantic principles. The majority of the houses were erected in view of magnificent landscapes, and they are where the leading figures of the day were born and raised.

Unjoru, the home of the Munhwa Ryu Clan, is located in Omi-ri, Toji-myeon, Gurye-gun, Jeollanam-do.The house is 99 *kan* in size, one *kan* being the space between four pillars. The site is considered to beone of the most auspicious in the entire country. Geomancers rated it so highly because, according to legend, this is where a heavenly maiden threw down a golden ring from Hyeongje Peak on Jirisan Mountain. A woman taking off a ring signified pregnancy, which in turn signified having lots of children and enjoying wealth and prosperity in agricultural society. Yi Gil-sun, who was 70 years old when I visited, is the wife of the ninth heir in the line of Ryu I-ju. She passed along what she had heard from her father-in-law about why the *jongga* had settled here:

He told me that the site is beautiful for five reasons.

> First, the mountain spreading like a folding screen behind the house shields us from the wind. Second, the candlestick-shaped peak illuminates our hearts. Third, the five peaks stretching out in front of us resemble five prime ministers bowing down. Fourth, the waters of the Seomjingang River and the streams flowing down Jirisan Mountain meet to make the soil rich in front of our house. Fifth, the richness of the site makes us generous.

The Structural Grace of Unjoru

Unjoru was built in 1776, during the reign of King Yeongjo (r. 1724–1776), by Ryu I-ju (1726–1797), who was the governor of Nakan-gun at the time. Exclaiming that heaven had kept the land for him, he enlisted several hundred young men to clear the rocky, barren terrain and then had his family settle there. The 99-*kan* house was built on a 4,630m^2 plot of land with 900 m^2 of floor space and a tiled roof. The various buildings were arranged in the shape of the Chinese character 品 (pronounced *pum*), symbolizing the dignity (*pumgyeok*) of the *seonbi*. The beauty of the landscape seen from the high porch on the men's quarters gave the house its romantic name, Unjoru, literally bird-in-cloud. From the moment I entered the compound, the space enchanted my eyes and heart. The water in the melodious brook that flowed in front of the lofty gate was so clear you could have drunk it straight from the ladle. With a stream flowing down from Wangsiru Peak (1,212 m), located northeast of the house and passing in front of the gate, this was surely a propitious spot, I thought. Even more remarkably, the family told me that the stream never overflowed its banks, even during the rainy season. The home was registered as Important Folk Property No. 8 in 1968.

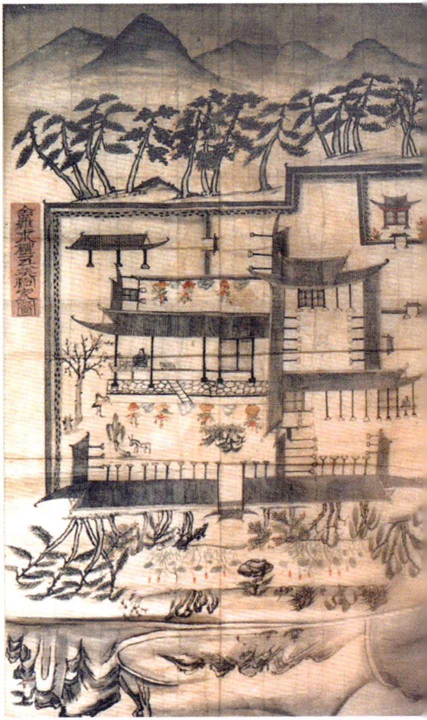

Jeollaguryeohmidonggado describes Unjoru, focusing on the auspiciousness of the location and its architectural structure and gardens that tries to enhance its advantage.

Unjoru's Rice Chest

Many stories are told about one particular object at Unjoru. At the entrance to the women's quarters is a round rice chest carved from a log, one that's big enough to hold at least two bags of rice. The bottom of the chest has a hole with a plug that says, "Other people can open me." The implication is that anyone who is hungry can open the lid and take some rice. The chest is a family tradition that was been kept since the lifetime of Ryu I-ju. This sentiment illustrates the family's sense of *noblesse oblige*, which inspired each generation to pay heed to the hardship of their neighbors and to put into practice the values of sympathy and sharing.

It was this sympathy for the suffering of other people represented by the rice chest that kept Unjoru safe while countless other buildings in the vicinity were burned during the Donghak Peasant Revolution, Japanese colonization, and the Korean War. The generations of people who were able to satisfy their hunger thanks to the rice in the chest quietly ensured the house's safekeeping during times of strife and turmoil.

There is also a diary at the home that the heir of each generation has kept for the past 150 years. The journal is considered extremely valuable as both an example of the development of an aristocratic family and a record of the experiences of this family in particular.

Pungsan Ryu Clan, Ryu Seong-ryong Jongga: Yangjindang and Chunghyodang

One of the best-known *jongtaek* is the home of Ryu Seong-ryong (1542–1607; pen name: Seo-ae)in Hahoe Village in Andong. If you visit Ryu Seong-ryong's home, known as Chunghyodang, you will see another old house separated from it by a single lane, this one called Yangjindang. Because of the beauty and age of the two houses, they have both been designated as national treasures. At first glance, it would be easy to think they are the same property, but in fact they belong to two separate *jongga*.

Yangjindang has been the greater *jongga* of the Pungsan Ryu Clan (and Chunghyodang the lesser) since they settled there 600 years ago, and it was the home of Ryu Un-ryong (1539–1601; pen name: Gyeom-am), the older brother of Ryu Seong-ryong. The two brothers got along so well they didn't mind being neighbors.

The Auspicious Site that Gave Birth to Distinguished Figures

The geography book *Taengniji* (The Elements of a Good Place to Live), written by Yi Jung-hwan during the reign of King Yeongjo, lists four requirements for selecting a place to live: an advantageous location, profitable land, human emotions, and a beautiful landscape. One place that was said to satisfy all four of these conditions was Hahoe Village. With their extensive knowledge

Chunghyodang is the lesser *jongga*, but it's not any lesser in the beauty of its architecture.

Men of *jongga* spend time at *daechungmaru*, the balcony area of Chunghyodang.

about the influence of the land and the stars, Joseon scholars were not about to overlook a site that was so auspicious. The current site of Yangjindang was chosen by Ryu Jong-hye, seventh in the line of the Pungsan Ryu Clan, who served as the minister of works in the early period of the Joseon Dynasty. Ryu, we are told, took 100 trips up Hwasan Mountain, which is behind Hahoe Village, searching for an auspicious site as carefully as if he were selecting the site of the royal palace; surely it is no coincidence that so many distinguished figures were born here. Ryu Un-ryong was a civil servant that the government recognized for his spotless integrity, while Ryu Seong-ryong made his name as the chief state councilor during the Imjin War (1592–1598). Hahoe Village, the site of the two houses, has been home to many members of the Pungsan Ryu Clan for 600 years, a legacy that continues through to the present day.

The Beauty of Hahoe Village

The village is surrounded on three sides by Hwasan Mountain, Namsan Mountain, and Wonjisan Mountain, like a folding screen. When the southward flowing Nakdonggang River reaches the village, it makes a gentle curve to the northeast, enfolding the village and weaving around the mountains. With superb natural scenery, including the bend of the river, unique rock formations, the endless reaches of sand, and the thick pine grove known as Mansongjeong, as well as age-old traditions, the village is as beautiful as an Asian landscape painting.

Aside from its geographic features, Hahoe Village is also famous for its unique cultural offerings, one of which being a mask dance traditionally performed as a means of mocking the upper class. This historical Korean village was registered as a World Cultural Heritage site by UNESCO in 2010, along with Yangdong Village in Gyeongju. Hahoe Village is one of the last remaining examples of the Korean traditional way of life.

The beautiful scenery of Hahoe Village

Wolseong Son Clan, Sonso Jongga: A House That Prince Charles Admired

Gyeongju, a city in the south of the Korean peninsula, is the site of Yangdong Village, one of the few places faithfully preserving the customs and homes of the Korean aristocracy. Living in the village are numerous descendents of two of Korea's most famous *jongga*: the Wolseong Son Clan and the Yegang Yi Clan. In 1992, Prince Charles of Britain stopped by the village and offered praise, which drew attention of the world.

Strangely enough, the village was not built on flat ground, but rather atop a steep hill. Another distinctive characteristic is that its old-fashioned tile-roofed houses are located at the highest point of the hill—the hardest point to reach. Why on Earth would these houses have been built on the side of a hill instead of on the rich fields of the wide Angang Plain?

The answer is perhaps unsurprising: The location was chosen because the area is believed to be an auspicious site. The site of a home needed to meet certain requirements in order for a great person to be born there, it was believed. In front of the village, there was to be a hill called Ansan; to the left and right, mountains shaped like a blue dragon and a white tiger, and to the rear, a low hill to shield it from the wind. All of these requirements were met at Yangdong Village, a site that nature had blessed. The front of the village was sheltered by a hill and lapped by the water of the Allakcheon stream; to its left and right mountains loomed like guardian spirits.

The Site Awaiting the Birth of Another Great Man

When the Wolseong Son Clan chose to build their home here, a geomancer declared it to be an auspicious site at which three

Jongson reads in peace sitting under the signboard which bears the house's name, Seobaekdang.

illustrious figures would be born, nourished on the energy emitted from Munjang Peak, located behind the village. Just as the prophecy dictated, two distinguished figures have been born into the family so far. One was Song Jung-don (1463–1529; pen name: U-jae), who served as a model for the Gyeongsang school of Confucian scholars in the early period of the Joseon Dynasty. The other was Yi Eon-jeok (1491–1533; pen name: Hoe-jae), Song Jung-don's nephew, who is honored today as one of Korea's five sages. The family looks forward to another great person being born in the family in the future.

Song Jung-don passed the government examination at the tender age of 27. While he was the governor of Sangju, he looked after the people under his care and was so highly regarded that they built a shrine for him while he was still alive. As a sign of his admiration for Song Jung-don's virtue, King Jungjong (r. 1506–1544) declared

Queen Elizabeth visited Hahoe Village in 1999 and her son, Prince Charles visited Yangdong Village during his visit at 1992. Both villages have been named by UNESCO as World Heritage sites.

him to be a person of unmatched integrity and bestowed upon him the posthumous epithet of Gyeongjeolgong. The king also gave Song's family special permission to keep his memorial tablet in the family shrine instead of burying it, and to offer ancestral rites for him in perpetuity. This rare honor, known as *bulcheonwi*, was accorded to those who had made a great contribution to the state or who were renowned for their learning and virtue.

A House More Than 500 Years Old

The home of the Wolseong Son Clan is an elegant building that is made of wood, a rare quality for a family residence that is more than 500 years old. The men's quarters and the women's quarters,

Members of Pungsan Ryu Clan observe ancestral rite at Yangjindang, Hahoe Village. Yangdong and Hahoe are the two villages where these rites are held in full formality.

which are built on a site commanding an excellent view of the village below, are linked together in the shape of a square. Rather that emphasizing the dignity of the men's quarters by keeping it separate from the women's quarters, the two are placed closely together, suggesting conjugal harmony. A juniper that was planted to mark the building of the house is registered as Local Cultural Property No. 8. When the branches of the tree are trimmed every few years, the descendents share the lumber, using it to make furniture for family members. Family members say that the furniture passed down in this way makes them proud to have such an illustrious ancestor.

Yecheon Kwon Clan, Kwon Mun-hae Jongga: The Birthplace of Korea's First Encyclopedia

Daesojae is a building that belongs to a time-honored *jongga* located in Jukrim-ri, Yongmun-myeon, Yecheon County, North Gyeongsang Province. The building has been declared a national treasure, an unusual honor for a house. But there are treasures to be found inside the house as well. The site is the storage place of the original draft of *Daedongunbugunok*, Korea's first encyclopedia, and 677 wooden block prints of the draft, as well as the diary of Kwon Mun-hae (1534–1591; pen name: Cho-gan).

Ancient Building with Hidden Artistic Sentiments

Daesojae is nestled in a village inhabited by a great number of members of the Yecheon Kwon Clan. Sitting at the base of a low hill that stretches out behind the property, the home is surrounded by wide fields. A 480-year-old juniper tree at the entrance to the compound symbolizes the family's long history, and the building located on the right as you step inside the compound is Daesojae, the men's quarters, the building that has been designated as national treasure. The latter was built during the lifetime of Kwon Mun-hae's grandfather, a man who served as the chief scholar under King Seonjo. It was declared a national treasure because so few houses built before the Imjin War have remained intact.

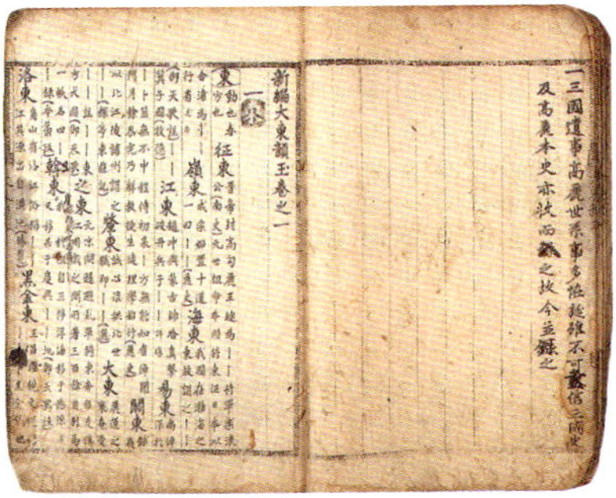

The twenty volumes of *Daedongunbugunok* cover extensively the history, geography, literature, even zoology and botany of early Joseon.

The house is surrounded with a railing and is built on an

Kwon O-sang, Kwon Mun-hae's grandfather is said to have built this building, a *byeoldang* (a building detached from the main house) called Daesojae. Its distinctive *daechungmaru* (the balcony area) provided open space for clan meetings and rituals that was essential to a *jongga*.

embankment that was raised to prevent the mountain from being harmed. From the outside, the building looks plain, but if you look at the roof from the 6-*kan* porch, the artistic sentiment of the family becomes apparent. Atop the ridge beam are props shaped like lotus leaves, and it is adorned with exquisite statuary. The women's quarters, which combine scale with functionality, have also been designated as an important folk property.

A Life of Dedication

The 13th head of the family is Kwon Yeong-gi. He was born in the women's quarters of the house, and though he is nearly seventy

years old, he has never lived outside the house. This man, who has dedicated his entire life since graduating from university to looking after his home and taking care of his family, is in some ways a cultural property himself. Rather than being annoyed by the people who come to see such a renowned figure, he is happy to see them. Because of the frequent visits to the house by foreign scholars, not to mention Koreans, Kwon and his wife serve as de facto cultural ambassadors. Kwon and his wife live inside a building that has been called a national treasure, but it occurs to me that there are treasures inside them as well.

Choganjeong Pavilion

Choganjeong Pavilion, said to have been built in 1582, when Kwon Mun-hae was 49 years old, is situated in the midst of beautiful scenery, next to a stream that flows between Mae Peak and Guksa Peak. Having been built on a base of rough stones piled on a natural stone slab in the stream, the pavilion embodies Kwon's ambition of creating a space that would harmonize people and nature. When climbing the pavilion, visitors are given the impression that they are floating above the water. The distinctive rocks and trees in bloom around the pavilion are enough to inspire poetry, and indeed, the pavilion often hosted poetry readings for literary-minded *seonbi* during the Joseon Dynasty, including Kim Seong-il, Jeong-gu, and Yi I, who were all intimate friends of Kwon. The pavilion is also said to be the spot where Kwon wrote the *Daedongunbugunok*, and where he wrote in his diary every day without fail for 10 years.

Choganjeong during the summer: cliffs and mountain tops were favored spots to build pavilions on.

Jongga Where Children Are Raised to Be Courteous

Another famous *jongga* whose descendents are still living at Yangdong Village alongside the Son family is that of Yi Eon-jeok, who was mentioned above. As a civil servant and Confucian thinker, Yi played an important role in the formation of the Gyeongsang faction of Confucian scholars in the 16th century during the Joseon Dynasty. He is one of the 18 sages who are housed at Munmyo, the shrine of Seonggyungwan in Seoul. Later scholars concluded that his creative interpretation of Confucianist thought was instrumental in developing Korea's own unique brand of neo-Confucianism.

A Jongga Where Children Live

The home in which the descendants of Yi Eon-jeok have lived for generations comprises a number of beautiful buildings that have been recognized as cultural treasures, including Mucheomdang and Hyangdan. But there is something else that adds to the house's charm: the warm smiles of the children who live there today. When I visited the house for my research, I was met by Jin-su and Jin-hyeon, the two sons of YiJi-rak, the 17thheir to the family line. With smiles on their faces, they bowed in a respectful greeting. In regard to their maturity and courtesy, the two children could easily have been members of the aristocracy during the Joseon Dynasty. They welcomed me even though I was a stranger, urging me to come out of the cold and up to the porch that was warmed by the sunlight. I was thankful that they remembered the small courtesy of carrying my bag.

Indeed, courtesy pervaded every move of the two children, which was appropriate, considering that they lived in a house that was considered a historical heritage. This was not courtesy that had been forced upon them, but rather behavior that they had picked up by living with adults. In the men's quarters, we could hear the head of the family reading a book aloud; in the women's

Mucheomdang, one of the most beautiful houses of Yangdong village is also one that children were raised in until recently, unlike most *jongga* nowadays.

quarters, his wife was preparing some refreshments. Much had changed over the centuries, but what I saw here was a natural expression of the spirit of the *jongga*—the value placed on learning, and the emphasis put on hospitality.

Beautiful Architecture Inspired by Filial Piety

Hyangdan is National Treasure No. 412. It was built by King Jungjong in 1543, while Yi Eon-jeok was governor of Gyeongsang Province, so that the governor could look after his ailing mother. Not only is the building gorgeous to look at from the outside, but it is also carefully laid out, with each section having its own purpose. There are several pavilions on the property as well, screened by a pine grove: Shimsujeong, Yeonggwijeong, Seolcheonjeongsa, and Yangjoljeong. Each of these pavilions has a name that is rich in meaning, and each of them was inspired by filial duty. The pavilions were built by various members of the family, as their circumstances allowed, both to commemorate the ancestors who had gone before them and to absorb each ancestor's noble spirit. They were sometimes used for teaching, and at other times as cultural sites where scholars held feasts in honor of the elderly.

Children raised in *jongga* naturally learn courtesy and especially the respect towards their elders.

5 Chapter Five

LEARNING: THE TEACHING AND PRACTICE OF MORAL PRINCIPLES

Koreans' fervor for education is well-known—even US President Barack Obama likes to talk about it. This passion for education, which is the engine driving Korea's economic development, is the product of the millennia-old ideology of Confucianism. By examining the mindset and educational culture of the *jongga*, we can learn about how this passion took root in Korean society and the implications of its legacy.

The Significance of Learning in Traditional Society

There were two reasons that learning was encouraged in traditional Korean society. The first of these was the idea that it was only through learning that one could become a complete individual. Confucian learning involves not only knowledge but moral precepts as well. In this way, the people of Joseon valued learning for its own sake. Through learning, they sought to acquire goals, commune with distinguished thinkers, and learn from their ideas so as to become scholars who could live a spiritual life and carry on the Confucian ideology. Although not all scholars would encourage their students to pursue success through service with the government, they still supported ongoing learning, recognizing that it enabled people to become scholars with the knowledge and capability of moral behavior.

The Only Way to Bring Glory to the Family

There was another reason for study, however. Because of the rigid caste system in the Joseon Dynasty, which divided society into scholars, farmers, craftspeople, and merchants, dedicating oneself to

Seodang is a village school where local *seonbi* taught students young and old the basics of Confucianism. Some still exist today and focus on teaching courtesy.

study and passing the civil service exam was essentially the only way to make a name for oneself and to bring glory to one's family. The emphasis on passing can perhaps be attributed to the incredible respect that Koreans have for reading and education formed during the five centuries of the Joseon Dynasty.

Education at the Jongga

In such a society, the heir to the family line needed to distinguish himself through his studies, not only for himself, but also for his family. Study was required for mastering the elaborate ancestral rites, while careful cultivation of Confucian moral behavior was essential for maintaining harmony in the family and for treating guests with the proper hospitality—the two things that were necessary for preserving the family name. The education in the *jongga* came into being with the goal of helping members of the family grow in this direction.

A reenactment of *gwageo*, the civil service exam in Joseon. The glory associated with passing of civil service exam often made it a lifelong goal for many sons of *jongga*, some of them taking it well into their sixties.

Jongga's Upbringing of a Child

Rather than direct instruction, education at these families was provided indirectly through the living environment. During their early years, boys were typically brought up in the women's quarters by their grandmother, who had a great deal of experience with taking care of young children. From the age of five or six, boys went to the men's quarters to stay with their grandfathers, where they learned the rudiments of education and studied textbooks for children. But reading was not the only skill they learned from their grandfather. There was much for the boys to learn from observing the behavior of their grandparents, which helped them develop self-control and a stable personality. It was in this way that children's daily lives trained them in the virtues of discipline and patience, the most important virtues for a Korean scholar.

Indeed, the education of young children in these families largely consisted of watching what their elders did and listening to what they said. Education of older children, on the other hand, varied according to the family's plans. Some children would stay at home to look after the land of their ancestors and to perform the ancestral rites, while others would be sent to study in Seoul. In Seoul, they could focus on preparing for the civil service exam, which would increase the family's level of prestige.

Toegye's grandson, Yi Young-do's *jongson* holds his granddaughter close. In a *jongga*, grandparents are central to the upbringing and nurturing of young children.

Putting Learning into Practice

The members of the *jongga*, who had been taught to be loyal and patient both through their studies and by their environment, were not eager to cause commotion. However, when the country was in danger, they often displayed a remarkable resilience and a spirit of sacrifice. In extreme cases this may have involved martyrdom, seen in Minister Bak Paeng-nyeon of the Suncheon Bak Clan, but was also bestowed upon those who made significant contributions to the independence movement, as was the case with nine members of the Yi Myeong Family of the Goseong Yi Clan. But even scholars who did not personally fight on the battlefield valiantly tried to preserve the spirit of the Korean people by collecting books and by maintaining the traditional way of life.

Ye, or propriety is about practice and resolve. Deep snow doesn't stop villagers of Wichon-ri from getting to the 400 years old Seollal (the Lunar New Year) bowing ceremony.

It is also worth noting how these Confucian households addressed the question of money. Though the *seonbi* did not think that being wealthy was wicked in and of itself, they did thinkthat an extravagant lifestyle could corrupt the mind and that it was wrong to profit from the misfortune of others. The self-discipline and sympathy for others that we see here are the source of the family rules followed by the Gyeongju Choi Clan, which, as discussed below, exercised restraint and benevolence while managing their good fortune.

守真居正

Gyeongju Choi Clan Saseonggong Jongga: Self-Discipline and Sympathy

The Rich Chois, as they are called, lived at No. 69 Gyo-dong in Gyeongju. The family was fabulously rich for 300 years, through 10 generations of the family. In addition to garnering attention for the riches of its members, the family is also famous for the incredible success it enjoyed in the civil service exam: The founder's heirs passed the exam for nine generations in a row. But the riches of this family went beyond the physical wealth of its members.

The newly restored *jongtaek* of Gyeonju Choi clan

A Truly Respected Family

There's a saying in Korea that seeing a cousin buy land gives you a bellyache, suggesting the envy we feel when other people succeed. This particular family, however, is bloodline to which the old proverb did not apply. When the Choi family bought more rice paddies, their neighbors were delighted—and not only the people in their own village, but people for miles around. The family even earned the admiration of people who, strictly speaking,had nothing to gain from them. The source of this respect was a set of rules drawn up by various members of the family for their descendants to follow. The rules encapsulated a set of life lessons learned by ancestors who came to understood that money is easier to make than to keep. These rules were summarized for me by Choi Yeom, the 11th heir to the family line, who is currently living in Seoul.

> Our family had six rules that have beenpassed down for three hundred years. First, don't go past the first level of the civil service exam. Second, don't own more land than is enough to grow 10,000 sacks worth of rice. Third, be hospitable to travelers. Fourth, don't buy any land in a lean year. Fifth, women who marry into the family should wear cotton clothes for their first three years. Sixth, don't let anyone living within 100 leagues of the house starve to death.

The Secret to Three Centuries of Prosperity

To the best of the family's ability, all six of these rules were kept. When Choi Yeom's mother came to the family house at the age of 16, she often had to skip meals. Guests were so frequent that she often had to put her own rice on guests' plate to ensure they had enough to eat. During one year, the family went through 1,000 sacks of rice feeding visitors who were staying in the men's quarters; that's how serious they were about being hospitable to travelers.

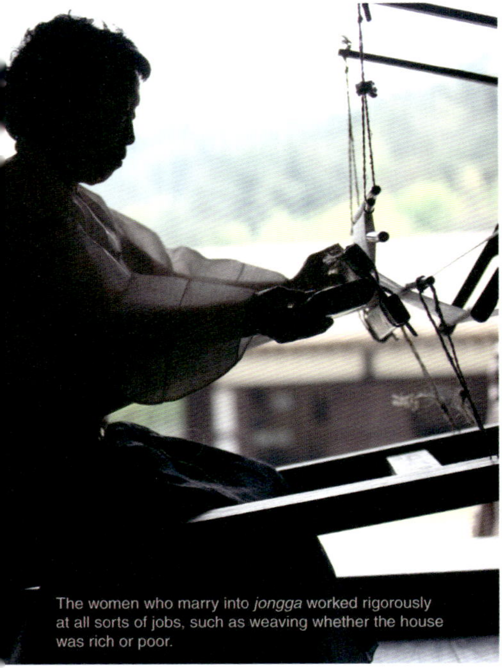

The women who marry into *jongga* worked rigorously at all sorts of jobs, such as weaving whether the house was rich or poor.

The family also faithfully adhered to the rule about not letting anyone starve to death within 40 kilometers of the house. When there was a poor harvest, the family would distribute food to the villagers, and family members never ate white rice which was considered a delicacy at the time. In addition, they used one-third of the revenue from tenant farmers to help the destitute. These rules fostered a spirit of sympathy in the family, teaching the principle that people must learn to work together.

The family rule about not advancing beyond the first civil service exam was instituted by Choi Jin-rip. Choi, a general who served with distinction during the Imjin War with Japan at the end of the 16th century and the second Manchu invasion of the country a few decades later, was the one who laid the foundation for the family's wealth. Choi came to believe that promotion to high office caused people to lust for wealth and power. For this reason, Choi urged his family members to only take the lowest level of the civil service examination, which served as a basic qualification for members of the aristocracy and would enable them to maintain the family's prestige, but stay out of political purge.

After Choi's death, his descendants applied themselves diligently to cultivating the land, while still treating their hired laborers and tenant farmers with generosity. As a result, only four generations after the esteemed general, family head Choi Ui-gi owned enough land for the family to fill 10,000 sacks of rice at each harvest, but in his last words he told the family to not expand their property beyond that. These two family rules embody the virtue of self-discipline.

Another rule of the family inspired by self-discipline and sympathy is the one about not buying land in a lean year. This is a rule that exemplifies the virtuous life, as well as the noble ethic of refusing to profit from the suffering of other people. This uncommon *noblesse oblige* is what that enabled the Choi family to protect their wealth for more than three centuries despite the numerous droughts that struck the region and the bandits roaming the countryside.

A *seom* is a unit used to measure rice, approximately 144 kilograms. Choi family's rice paddies brought in 10,000 *seom* after each harvest.

Women of Pyungsan Ryu Clan are working to pile rice cakes for a *bulcheonwi*.

Jongga's Education of Values Through Life

One final rule hints at the how the *jongga* continued to observe these rules for centuries. It shows how the home served as a place of education, enabling family members to internalize the family's values. This was the rule that women who had married into the family had to wear cotton clothes instead of silk for her first three years with the family. During this period, families saw a new wife as someone who needed to be educated in the customs of her new family. As such, having her wear cotton clothes for three years was meant to help her adjust to the thrift and self-discipline that were core values of the *jongga*, values that governed its way of life. In this way, the family ensured that family members would learn the right way to live through their everyday lives.

The Choi family eventually spent its entire fortune establishing Daegu University, and is not a wealthy family today. Nevertheless, the family's philosophy of self-discipline and empathy that was handed down by past generations is respected even more today and thought to be a model of *noblesse oblige* practiced during the Joseon Dynasty.

Daegu Seo Clan Seo Seong Jongga: Summoning the Courage to Seek Out Opportunity

For some *jongga*, bringing honor to one's ancestors was better served through the dedication to public office than looking after family home. Families of this sort sought opportunities for their heirs to move past being a member of the local gentry, seeking out connections and opportunities that would help male descendants stay abreast of the latest developments in learning. By sending their sons to be educated in the heart of Seoul, they could ensure that they would meet and get to know people of a similar social standing, some of whom would become lifelong friends. Families also saw this as a way to get the latest news from the capital. Even if their sons were unable to obtain a high government position, the friends they would make along the way would become a priceless asset, the parents believed.

This signboard at the old Andong house of Daegu Seo Clan says "the room of Yakbong's Birth," marking the signficance of their greatest ancester.

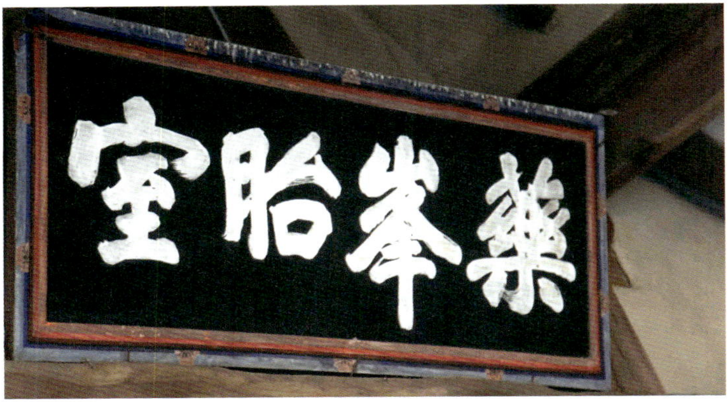

Seo Seong's mother, Yi understood well the importance of good food in attracting guests.

A Blind Widow's Commitment to Her Son's Success

Such thoughts is best exemplified in the family of Seo Seong (pen name: Yakbong), who dedicated himself to his studies after his mother relocated the family to Seoul 450 years ago. Seo's mother was Yi, a blind woman who married into the Sohoheon family in Andong, Gyeongsangbuk-do. When she lost her husband at the age of 21, after their son's first birthday, she decided that the only way to repay her beloved husband's generosity was by raising his son as best she could. With this sentiment in mind, she left the family home for Seoul,determined to provide the best education possible for her 3-year-old son. Having grown up in a distinguished family herself, Yi had learned at an early age that a house derives positive energy from having frequent visitors, and prepared many delicacies to serve to guests. A great deal of young Seo's academic development came from the opportunities he had as a child to interact with noted scholars and writers of the time who visited the house, perhaps drawn by the rumor of delicious cooking.

The Jongga with Most Illustrious Career

Yi's dedication did not go to waste. Her son Seo Seong went on to pass the highest level of the civil service exam and hold a series of powerful government positions, starting the family's own dynasty of civil service in the Joseon era. Some 140 of them passed the initial civil service exam, with dozens rising to high ranks in the government: 28 senior administrators, 15 deputy ministers, 34 ministers, 6 chief scholars, and 9 state councilors. The family was a veritable font of talent, an eminent bloodline if ever there was one, which could not have seen such remarkable success without the courageous decision made by Yi, Seo Seong's mother.

One value emphasized in the Seo Seong family is kindness. For generations, the family motto has been "don't neglect to be good," suggesting that family members should build up positive karma by helping those who are in trouble,

Passing the civil service exam and serving the country was seen as one of the greates honor a man could achieve.

that they should remain neutral regardless of the circumstances. This reasoning is perhaps what allowed so many members of the Seo Seong family to attain high office despite the numerous political purges during the Joseon Dynasty.

Goseong Yi Clan, Yi Myeong Jongga: Sacrificing Everything for the Nation

Imcheonggak in Beopheung-dong, Andong, Gyeongsangbuk-do, is the largest traditional house in Korea that is still inhabited today. It was once a 99-*kan* house, but about half of the house was torn down to lay a railroad during Japanese occupation. Even so, the building retains its grandeur. It is a rare example of an old family home that combines an imposing, austere exterior with the warm, welcoming interior more characteristic of Korea's traditional houses.

This house is located at Andong, the home of a great number of members of the Goseong Yi Clan. Situated among striking natural beauty, Imcheonggak and Gunjajeong Pavilion were built here by Yi Myeong, a high-ranking official in the justice ministry under King Jungjong (r. 1506–1544). Yi Myeong was the grandson of Yi Won, the chief state counselor under King Sejong (r. 1418–1450). Today, Imcheonggak is usually associated with Yi Myeong, the person who built it.

Yi Myeong's descendants excelled in their studies, and many of them went on to serve with distinction in the local government. Yi Sang-ryong (pen name: Seokju), who served as the first president of the Provisional Government of Republic of Korea in Shanghai, China, was born at Imcheonggak. This is a point of pride not only for the Goseong Yi clan but also for the people of Andong as a whole. The family has continually proven its patriotism, with Yi Sang-ryong and nine of his relatives receiving special recognition from the government of Korea.

The Provisional Government of Republic of Korea at Shanghai

Practicing Morality is More Important than Reading It

After Japan annexed Korea by force in 1910, Yi Sang-ryong said, "Put Confucius and Mencius back on the shelf. It won't be too late to read them after the nation has been saved." In 1911, he moved with his family and several others to Manchuria, where he started the independence movement. In Manchuria, the family established a local government and a military academy called Military School of the New Rising to train officers for the independence movement. This academy played a crucial role in the early stage of the independence movement and worked to instill a sense of nationalism in Koreans. Students at the academy were taught with a history textbook called *Great Eastern History*. The textbook, which was published by the school, shed new light on Korean history.

When the independence movement ran low on funds, Yi Sang-ryong went to great lengths to raise money, even selling Imcheonggak and other property that had been in the clan for 500

Seokju Yi Sang-ryong's portrait after being appointed as the first president of Korea's provisional government in Shanghai in 1925.

Yi Byeong-hwa (middle), Seokju's grandson was also a fervent freedom fighter.

years. Yi's great-grandson Yi Hang-jeung, who looks after Imcheonggak today, says that his ancestor could not have made that decision if it were not for his dedication to and passion for Korean independence. Yi believes that his ancestor's dedication was a significant source of inspiration for the independence movement.

The Persecution and Death of Independence-fighting Heirs

Yi Sang-ryong was elected as the first president of Korea's provisional government in Shanghai in 1925, but the following year he resigned from his post and returned to Jiandao, the area north of the Yalu River, where he worked to bring together the various independence groups operating in Manchuria. But after the Japanese set up the puppet state of Manchuko, pressure on the overseas independence movement intensified, and many of Yi's comrades in the movement were killed. Yi eventually refused to eat anymore, and his life came to a close at the age of 75. He had been

The burial ceremony of Yi Sang-ryong and other freedom fighters on 1994 was held as a national event.

living in exile for 21 years.

After Yi's death, his only son Jun-hyeong and his grandson Byeong-hwa returned with their families to their ancestral home of Imcheonggak. Although circumstances forced them to bury Yi's remains in Jiandao, they remained in mourning for three years. Since the Japanese had destroyed the family records and was keeping the descendants under close surveillance, they were unable to do anything. When Yi Sang-ryong's grandson Byeong-hwa was thrown into prison, Jun-hyeong, who had dedicated his entire life to helping his father Sang-ryong and supporting the independence movement, was filled with despair. He ended his own life at the age of 67, believing that living one more day in a country ruled by a foreign power would only add to his shame.

Yi Hang-jeung points to his ancestor's last words. Yi Sang-ryong urged the people to fight for freedom despite all oppression.

Commemorating People Who Lived Up to Their Beliefs

Three years later, Korea was freed from the Japanese occupation, but competing ideologies in the northern and southern parts of the country soon led to the Korean War. Byeong-hwa had been beaten down by the torture he endured as an independence fighter, and he died of a broken heart before the age of 50. Both Byeong-hwa and his father Jun-hyeong were posthumously awarded the Order of Merit for National Foundation, and today their remains are interred at Daejeon National Cemetery.

The six sons of Byeong-hwa lived during a tumultuous period of history. With three having died during occupation and one going missing during the Korean War, in 1962, the two remaining brothers went to Jiandao to bring back the remains of their great-grandfather Yi Sang-ryong, and laid them to rest at the Seoul National Cemetery.

The members of the family from Imcheonggak demonstrate that the meaning of learning is not found in the pages of a book, but rather in how it is applied through action. By willing to risk everything to live according to their principles, they exemplify the true spirit of the *seonbi*.

APPENDIX

INFORMATION

Books on Jongga by the Author

Lee, Yeonja. *Stories of Jongga That Has Continued for a Thousand Years*. Seoul: Cultureline, 2001.

Lee, Yeonja. *In the Search of Jongga*. Seoul: Cultureline, 2002.

Lee, Yeonja. *The Story of Jongga*. Seoul: Cultureline, 2004.

Lee, Yeonja. *The People of Jongga*. Seoul: Random House Joongang, 2005.

Lee, Yeonja. *Wisdom in the Life of Jongga*. Seoul: RHK, 2012.

References

Chun, Byeong-june. *Understanding Korean Traditional Rituals through Zhu Xi's Family Rituals*. Seoul: Korean Studies Information, 2012.

Jeon, Jinmun. *The Secret to Three Hundred Years of Wealth*. Seoul: Minumin, 2004.

Huh, Eun. *I Still Hear the Howling Winds of Manchuria*. Seoul: Jungwoosa, 1995.

Yi Soon-hyung. *Korea's Jongga*. Seoul: Seoul National University Press, 2000.

Oh, Hong-seok. *Traditional Korean Villages*. Seoul: Ewha Womans University Press, 2009

Zhu Xi. *Family Rituals*. Trans. Yim Minhyuk. Seoul: Yeamun Seowon, 1999

Yi Joong-hwan and Bak Jega. *Taekliji and Bukhakyui*, Trans. Noh Doh-yang, Yi Seok-ho, Seoul: Daeyang Books, 1973.

National Folk Museum. *Korea's Funeral Rituals*. Seoul: Mijinsa, 1990.

Yi Joong-hwan. *Taekliji*. Trans. Yi Yikseong, Seoul: Hangilsa, 1992.

Korean Studies Advancement Center Editors. *Asking the Meaning of Confucianism Today*. Seoul: Korean Studies Advancement Center, 2011.

Some content of this book has been compiled, edited, and supplemented by Lee Yeonja and Kim Mira from the following articles published in:

KOREANA Vol. 24. No1. Spring 2010
"What Is the Significance of Jongga in Korea's Modern-day Society?" by Yi Soon Hyung

KOREANA Vol. 26 No 1.Spring 2012
"Karen Kim: "There Is a Spirituality to Korean Clan Culture" by Charles La Shure

Chapter 2, 3, 4, and 5 were newly written by authors Lee Yeonja and Kim Mira.

PHOTOGRAPHS

Lee Dong Chun 10, 20, 22, 29, 89, 91, 96

Park Tae Shin 30, 45, 54, 56, 59

Yonhap Photo 13, 14, 15, 24, 25, 35, 37, 39, 43, 45, 47, 51, 55, 58, 60, 61, 63, 74, 75, 77, 83, 85, 88, 90, 92, 94, 95, 98, 99, 100, 102, 103, 104

KTO 5, 6, 17, 18, 21, 27, 32, 33, 40, 41, 42, 44, 49, 50, 53, 55, 56, 65, 76, 78, 81, 82, 87, 94, 98, 105, 106

Cultural Heritage Administration 67, 69, 70, 71, 72, 79, 80, 84

Image Today 52

Credits

Publisher	Kim Hyung-geun
Writer	Lee Yeonja, Kim Mira
Translator	David Carruth
Editor	Hansol Kim
Copy Editor	Jaime Stief
Designer	Lee Bok hyun